In memory of Andrei Kapitsa

SERGEI KAPITSA

PARADOXES OF GROWTH

LAWS OF GLOBAL DEVELOPMENT OF HUMANITY

GLAGOSLAV SCHOLARS

PARADOXES OF GROWTH

by Sergei Kapitsa

Translated by Inna Tsys

Edited by Scott Moss and Huw Davies

Interior Layout by Dmitry Podolyanchuk

Cover by Max Mendor

© 2010, Sergei Kapitsa

© 2017, Glagoslav Publications, United Kingdom

Glagoslav Publications Ltd
88-90 Hatton Garden
EC1N 8PN London
United Kingdom

www.glagoslav.com

ISBN: 978-1-78267-121-3

A catalogue record for this book is available from the British Library.

CONTENTS

A Note from the Author..7

Acknowledgements..11

In Search of a Model for the Growth of Humanity...............13

    Introduction..13

    Modeling Humanity's Global Growth...............23

    The Demographic Revolution........................38

    The Growth of World Population...............43

    The Transformation of Time in History...............50

    The Problem of Time in History........................53

    Breaks and Demographic Transitions...............57

    Birth Rate, Aging, Migration........................70

What Does the Model for Understanding History Give Us?......78

    Energetics and Economics of Humanity...............78

    Demographic Revolution and the Crisis of Ideology...............84

    Science, Innovation and Society........................89

    Socio-economic Consequences of Growth...............95

    Stability of Growth and System-Defined Crisis...............101

    Russia in the Global Context........................107

    General Positions and Conclusions...............112

    Conclusion..114

Appendix..120

    A Mathematical Theory of Population Growth...............120

A Note from the Author

The very first time you meet someone you are always interested to know how old they are, and depending on who you see before you—a little boy, a young woman, a venerable elder—your attitude toward each of them will be different. Thereafter, you might be interested in the composition of the person's family, how many brothers and sisters your interlocutor has. When you travel to a different city or country, you will want to find out what the population there is like. Now, if our planet were to be visited by an alien, his first question upon encountering us would undoubtedly be: how many people are there here and how long have they been living here? This book is dedicated specifically to this eternal cycle of questions.

We will search for the answers to them with the help of a quantitative and complex study of the history and the foreseeable future of humanity. For this purpose the author drew on the facts presented by demographics, in which the object of research is the quantity of the population of the countries of the world. Contained within information about the number of people on Earth are the results of the social, economic and cultural undertakings of history, which opens up the opportunity for a collective analysis of humanity's history. When we analyze this problem, all of humanity is viewed as a single object, as one developing system. The model of growth itself is based on the methods and images of physics and refers to mathematics for a description of data from the past. However, the connection between the growth of the world's population and the duration of development cannot be grasped without taking into account the relativity of historical time—when one's own scale of time in history is compressed by tens of thousands of times as a result of this development.

In light of this acceleration of growth, the sources of the global demographic revolutions that all of humanity is currently experiencing become more understandable. A critical transition from explosive growth to constant quantity is tied to contemporary and critical issues about the lives of the people: the falling birth rate and global safety, the systemic and financial crisis and changes to the model of development itself during the transition to societal knowledge.

The modern era is marked by a change in our history, a demographic revolution, and calls for a new level of generalization and synthesis. It is therefore of interest to appeal to scientific concepts which presumptuously describe themselves as exact and quantitative, despite the fact that during the study of the growth of humanity throughout history, details about development in space and time are inevitably lost, and the picture of past events only provides a rough description of the past. With such a logical, quantitative approach to the description of history, difficulties in marrying it to the traditions of social sciences naturally arise. However, the author hopes that this experience of an interdisciplinary understanding of history will prove to be useful and fruitful. In an epoch of sudden shifts, the discussion of issues of global safety presents itself as particularly pertinent.

Physicists have created a weapon that is capable of destroying all of humanity. It is time they and society recognized the consequences of thoughtless arms races as a dead-end path to conflict resolution, the need to assume responsibility for understanding its consequences, and the need to stop.

In the modern world, the global crisis is reflected in the fact that, on all levels, economic power itself doesn't correspond to our social development and management, as can be observed in the way our actions and thoughts diverge. Nevertheless, the author hopes that this book will help with the interaction between the two most important forces, in the shape of our mind and our material development, which, for Russia, is particularly pertinent.

Finally, the fully developed approach in this book enables us to analyze the contemporary global systemic crisis, which so suddenly but not unexpectedly befell mankind. There is strong reason to believe that the demographic revolution, during which there is a sharp transition from exploding growth to the stabilization of the population, is the reason for the global crisis of a growing population and economic development.

It is here that the true source of the crisis and the urgent worldwide changes in our epoch can be found. In our country M.S. Gorbachev was called upon to solve these problems. His response to the challenge of the time was a call to engage in a *"new way of thinking"* in an epoch of rapid changes, changes over which those who had initiated them had already lost their power.

The author's interest in this range of problems arose during his participation in the Pugwash Conferences on Science and World Affairs and in discussions about the dangers of nuclear war, and later in the work of the Club of Rome, when the importance of research into global problems was acknowledged with particular clarity. It soon became clear that the dynamic of the Earth's population growth provided the key to these things.

However, the development of this field of study was not immediately understood or accepted. A first article, *Phenomenological Theory of the Population Growth of Earth*, was published in the magazine *Progress of Physical Sciences* (v. 106, #1, 1996), and an explanation of the conclusions it contained was given in the last article, *To the Theory of the Growth of Population of Earth* (UFN (Uspekhi Fizicheskikh Nauk), v. 180, #12, 2010). Details of these conclusions, **data about** anthropology and history and bibliographical references can also be found in published works and the report which was presented to the Club of Rome and published in 2007 [3].

The book is addressed to all who are interested in this problem but aren't experts; hence it has been adapted so that it can be understood by readers from various professional backgrounds. The book consists of three parts. In the first part, the concept of the model is examined and an account of the basic results of mathematical simulation, which led to the theory of the growth of the world's population, is given. In the description of this model, anthropological and historical views and data are touched upon, to the extent that the quantitative information required in order to construct the theory itself and provide a basis for it is contained within them.

The second part is dedicated to an interpretation of the development and history of humanity, and later the author turns to the present and to the future that may be in store for us. This discussion of global problems does not lay claim to fullness of analysis. Its goal is to show the possibilities opened by a collective analysis of world history, based on an examination of the population of Earth as a single system. This is the central thesis of the entire concept developed by the author.

In the third part, the collective theory of the growth of humanity and all the calculations required for it are set out. This part can be omitted during a first reading. For the sake of fullness and persuasiveness during the recounting of interdisciplinary problems, the author took the liberty of repeating the essential ideas and conclusions.

Author's e-mail: *sergey.kapitza@gmail.com*

Acknowledgements

The development of these studies would not have been possible without collaboration with colleagues from several different fields of study. I am indebted to G.I. Barenblatt for giving me an understanding of auto-model processes, A.G. Vishnevskiy and N.M. Rimashevskaya, who introduced me to the issues and methods of demography and assisted in a fruitful discussion at the Institute of Demography. I am thankful to L.I. Abalkin, V.L. Makarov, R.N. Aetnov and Kondratiev's Fund for the attention and support I received from the Russian Academy of Sciences (RAS). To A.U. Shevyakov—I am grateful for his support and understanding, when he invited me to the Institute of Socio-Economic Problems of Population of the RAS, and if not for his untimely passing our collaboration would have continued. The attention of historians V.S. Myasnikov and A.O. Chubaryan and support from A.A. Kokoshin and V.S. Stepin was very considerable. I am grateful to the President of RAS, U.S. Osipov, for his assistance and for giving me the opportunity to speak at the conference of the Presidium of RAS.

A discussion of these results took place at conferences and meetings at Moscow State University, and I am obliged to V.A. Sadovnich for his understanding and support. Support and development of our work was also contributed by S.P. Kurdumov and a team from the Institute of Applied Mathematics led by M.V. Keldish; our research was recognized with an award from the Russian Republic in the year 2000.

Appearances at the Universities of Amsterdam, Groningen, Eindhoven, Stockholm, Dresden, Cottbus, St. Petersburg and Prague were essential. A demonstration in the Kurchatov Institute, the Joint Institute for Nuclear Research, the European Organization for Nuclear Research (EONR), Massachusetts Institute of Technology, the National Laboratory of Los Alamos and Santa Fe Institute provided the opportunity to speak before an audience of physicists. Participation in projects by Terra-2000 and UNESCO (United Nations Educational, Scientific and Cultural Organization), Pugwash Conferences and meetings of the Club of Rome were also helpful.

Participation in the Davos Forum, the European Business Congress and a presentation at the annual meeting of Deutsche Bank provided for the understanding of the interests of business circles. I am grateful to the Chancellor of the Russian New University, V.A. Zernov, and our colleagues at the Nikitsky Club, who provided a unique audience for a discussion of the global range problem. The author is obliged to the Moscow Interbank Currency Exchange, to N.M. Rumyantseva for unfailing assistance, to Irena Seregina, and also to the editor E.V. Chudinova for the attention she showed during her work on this book. Thanks also to UNESCO, the Royal Society of London, Cambridge University, INTAS (The International Association for the Promotion of Co-operation with Scientists from the New Independent States of the Former Soviet Union) and the RFBR (Russian Foundation for Basic Research) funds and the Fund of D.B. Zimin *Dynasty*, to which I am obliged for their support at different stages of my work.

I am grateful to Zh. I. Alferov, A.I. Ageev, A.A. Akaev, K.V. Anuhin, V. Vaiskopf, N. N. Vorontsov, O.V. Viugin, O.G. Gazenko, V.F. Galetskiy, A.V. Gaponov-Grehov, I.M. Gelfand, R.S. Grinberg, P. Dzhonston, A.V. Derevyanko, I.M. Diyakonov, A.D. Zhukov, D.B. Zimin, V.V. Ivanov, B.B. Kadomtsev, N. Kaifitsu, A. Kingu, I. Koppen, U.L. Klimontovich, M.V. Kovalchuk, A.B. Kurzhanskiy, E.S. Kurkina, N.P. Laverov, G.V. Manelisu, G.G. Malinetskiy, G.I. Marchuk, G.A. Mesyats, N.N. Moiseev, I.V. Perevozchik, V.M. Polterovich, G. Prins, L.P. Pitaevskiy, I.R. Prigozhin, F.Y. Radermaher, M. Riz, D. Rotblat, U.A. Rizhov, V.A. Tishkov, E.A. Tonch, D.I. Trubetskiy, A.B. Usmanov, V.E. Fortov, D. Holdren, H. Shopper, V.A. Shuper, A.M. Chetto, El Hasan bin Talal, V.I. Yakunin and A.L. Yanshin for their understanding and support.

In Search of a Model for the Growth of Humanity

Introduction

This study is based on a quantitative description of humanity as a dynamic system. Its growth and development are bound to the interaction that grips all people: coming into existence with the appearance of man, with the gift of consciousness. It is no wonder that Aristotle's (384–322 BC) major work *Metaphysics* begins with the assertion that "All men by their nature strive for knowledge."

It is specifically our developed conscience, language, and culture that make us fundamentally different from other mammals, which is why there are a hundred thousand times more of us than there are animals commensurate to us. In essence, this particular study of the growth of humanity as a global problem is dedicated to this question.

Work on this issue led to the proposal of a quantitative model of growth and development [1, 2, 3]. It was not very clear, however, why this model, the mathematical means of which are so very simple, not to say elementary, turned out to be so substantial and effective. Therefore, not only is the model of human population growth presented in this article, but it also shows how the results are supported by views of anthropology and history, and how they compare to the conclusions presented by economics and an analysis of the stability of development. Thus the presentation is dedicated not so much to the conclusions of the fundamental mathematical equations as to a clarification of the circumstances of their adherence to the reality and views of the other sciences, primarily the social ones.

Thomas Malthus[1] was the first to address this cycle of questions. Despite the fact that he studied in the theological department of the University of Cambridge, he had a strong knowledge of mathematics. During my visit to his memorial office at Jesus College, I noticed the role that the writings of Leonhard Euler[2] had played. This great mathematician developed mathematical analysis in such a way that we recognize it even now as a reliable tool for physicists and engineers. Malthus mastered it fully—it was no accident that he came ninth in the University Mathematical Olympiad in 1783. I was of the hope, therefore, that contemporary social scientists would also be able to master mathematics at the level demonstrated by the author of the first model of population growth.

Malthus' approach and worldview is directly related to the development of classical mechanics in the eighteenth century, and served as a response to the mechanical Newtonian methodology and the views of the epoch of the Enlightenment. He was influenced by the views of the Physiocrats, who maintained that agriculture and the production of produce define the development of society. Malthus' own proposal, to the effect that the exponential growth of the population is limited by resources, defined all the subsequent development of similar studies for a long time to come.

The last reference to such an approach was the first presentation to the Club of Rome[3] of *The Limits of Growth* [4]. In 1972, following the ideas of the American scientist Jay Forrester[4] about the mathematical modeling of complex systems, the authors of this presentation, under the leadership of Dennis Meadows[5], having analyzed a broad database, attempted to describe the current development of humanity. The basis of the lecture was a simulation of the global process of growth as the sum of its component parts. Thus attention was drawn to these global problems,

---

[1] English priest and scientist, demographer and economist.

[2] Swedish, German, and Russian mathematician and mechanic

[3] The global 'think tank' that deals with a variety of international political issues

[4] Known as the founder of the System Dynamics, which deals with the simulation of interactions between objects in dynamic systems

[5] A former director of the Institute for Policy and Social Science Research at the University of New Hampshire

which represents a great achievement by the authors of the first lecture to the Club of Rome. However, the results, based upon a reductionist policy in adding up the factors of growth, revealed all the limitations of linear models and, consequently, of the concept of resource limitation of human population growth.

In this respect, the remarks of the American economist, Nobel Prize laureate Herbert Simon, are of particular interest:

> Forty years of experience modeling complex systems on computers, which with each passing year were becoming larger and faster, taught us that brute force would not lead us along a royal path to an understanding of such systems... Thus, modeling will demand reliance on fundamental principles, which will lead us to a solution to this paradox of such complexity.

The current work is a response to this challenge. Indeed, an integrated description of humanity leads us to the conclusion that social processes of development are directly related to the growth of the population. However, this is a non-linear connection, in which there is no simple cause and effect of growth and development. Therefore, such an approach is possible only if we examine the whole of humanity as an interconnected whole.

In this view of things, the position of the majority of prominent modern historians, such as Fernand Braudel, Karl Jaspers, Immanuel Wallerstein, Igor Diakonoff, and Nikolai Conrad, who affirmed that a true understanding of human development is possible only on a global level, is important. To a large extent, they developed a holistic view of global history, which became an essential premise for studies of this kind, in which the development of mankind was examined from the very beginning.

It's no wonder that the Academician Conrad wrote in his final collection of articles, *East and West* (1972):

> Thus, the knowledge that we have of the past combined with what our modern science opens to us with regard to the past and also the future, allows us to interpret the course of the historical life of humanity and by this means outline a philosophical concept of history. This is only possi-

ble, however, by paying attention to the history of all of mankind, and not to particular groups of peoples or countries…

> The body of evidence suggesting that human history is the history of all mankind and not of individual nations and countries—and that to understand the process of history one must study the history of humanity—is huge, and is made up of facts from all areas of life. All of history is full of them" [8].

The German historian and philosopher, Karl Jaspers, in his book *The Meaning and Prescription of History* (1948), begins the first part of *Global History* with these words:

> By the width and depth of change in all human life, our epoch is of decisive significance. Only the history of humanity in its entirety can give us a scale for an understanding of what is going on in modern times[5].

Jaspers gives a detailed argument of the importance of an examination of the history of humanity as a global process, when all humanity as a whole becomes the object of research. He singles out processes of development, which span the entire world. However, historical science has come a long way in its knowledge of the general laws which determine the growth and development of humanity.

It should be noted that this search was not easy, since, just as in demography, the fragmentation of facts and circumstances in the continuously increasing multitude of particulars prevented these attempts from capturing the general patterns. It was no wonder that the distinguished economist Friedrich Hayek noted,

> The division of the study of society into specialized disciplines led to a situation in which all of the most essential questions were neglectfully cast into the margins of an unclear philosophy of the development of society.

The above-mentioned historians' views became the starting points in the approach to the growth of the world's population and the development of humanity as one whole, a developing dynamic system. However, in demography such a point of view was systematically denied, inasmuch as the task of demographics was viewed as linking population growth with the specific social and economic conditions in an individual country or region and on this basis giving recommendations on demographic policy. It was specifically this that hindered the acceptance of a global and phenomenological approach, and the conclusions that result from it, by demographers, as well as social scientists, who are conceptually bound by the borders of countries and by the traditions of their science.

It should be emphasized that the phenomenological approach is understood by us the way that it is accepted in physics, and not in philosophy. We appeal to the general principals of self-similar development, the causations expressed in statistical representation, and on this foundation we build a theory. We are not therefore referring to so-called elementary occurrences and factors, by summarizing which we can describe the whole. Experience shows that even for systems that are simpler than humanity, such an approach to building an effective model is often practically impossible.

The first and most successful experiment at a phenomenological approach was developed in thermodynamics, when gas was examined as a system made up of many interacting particles. Due to collisions between the molecules found in an isolated system in thermodynamic balance, their condition can change slowly and reversibly. In this case variables such as temperature and pressure can be introduced, determining the thermodynamic condition of the system, and we can also turn our attention to our ideas about energy and entropy, without going into a detailed understanding of the properties of the atoms or molecules of which gases are composed.

In the future, when studying the development processes of complex systems—open systems, far from equilibrium, in which irreversible processes of evolution and growth occur—it turns out that the phenomenological approach opens a path to understanding such systems on a new basis. Even for a system as complex as humanity, it enables us to describe the processes of growth and development of the Earth's population.

Only by attaining a global level of analysis and broadening the scale of the problem to examine the entire population of the world as a single entity, as an interconnected system, was it possible to describe the development of humanity as a whole. Furthermore, such a generalized understanding of history turned out to be not just possible, but also very effective. Not only can our past, including the most distant events, be described from this standpoint, but the global demographic transition we are currently experiencing can as well, and on this basis, one can propose a picture of our development in the foreseeable future. To this end, the method of research and point of view in both space and time had to be radically altered, and humanity had to be studied from its very beginnings, as a global structure.

> *"Only by looking at the entire population of the world as a single coherent system was it possible to describe the development of humanity as a whole."*

In this case, we should not look for the reason for growth in the sum of all the relevant factors, but in the collective interaction that envelopes all of humanity and determines its development. Furthermore, it became clear that the development of this dynamic system is not only non-linear and irreversible, but is also far from equilibrium, and that a demographic revolution is currently taking place. It is a phased transition into a new condition, in a physical sense specifically. Throughout history, humanity has never before experienced such a profound reconstruction of the system, and that is what makes our era so unique.

It should be noted that this approach has not been easily accepted. It was not for nothing that the great mathematician and physicist, the academician Ludvig Faddeev, discussing the author's paper at the Presidium of the RAS, astutely pointed out that every generation is usually convinced that it is exceptional. For that very reason he drew attention to the need for consistent affirmation of the conclusion drawn. This is indeed the author's objective, to a large extent. This is why we are going to draw on a phenomenological, holistic description of growth, and examine humanity as a single, highly-intertwined system, in which there is a control mechanism that governs development, and in this way we will understand what is happening. The understanding gained can then become the basis of our solutions and actions.

"Humanity has never before experienced reconstruction through a path of transition into a new condition."

The emergence of the system that we call humanity is the result of its *self-organization and evolution*, which led to its emergence as a qualitatively new object, separating it from the rest of the living world. This is why we refer to methods, using collective interactions for a description of causal relationships in the evolution of complex systems. By complex systems we mean systems, the development of which depends on the number of relationships between all the people on Earth. Then the extent of the complexity of the system is not determined by the total number of people, but in the first approximation of the quantity of the world's population squared. This is expressed by the nonlinearity of the process of growth and the impossibility of referring to simple cause-effect connections between growth and development.

"The passage of time in history is irregular and is dependent on the process of growth itself."

Furthermore, it transpires that the passage of time in history is irregular and depends on the process of growth itself. The compression of historical time strongly intensifies the rate of growth and adds a special significance to everything that is happening in our era of demographic revolution.

Thus, when interpreting the phenomenological theory of the growth of our planet's population, it is necessary to refer to ideas about the physics of non-linear occurrences and unbalanced processes, developed in the sciences of the 20th century, and right from the outset discard the additive and linear approach. It is important to note that a similar theory, hypothetically, must operate using statistic distributions for variables. But in the first instance, the author confined himself to a simplification, in which their average and effective values are input.

Referring to the idea of the complexity and interconnection of the system with which we describe the development of humanity, we pursued the goal of clarifying the meaning of the conclusions reached and identifying the limits of the extent to which they apply. As a result, we are following an approach developed in theoretical physics; this allows us to base our conclusions and effective theory on phenomenology, as opposed to the reductionism presented by additive linear models. Moreover, the basis of the theory takes human consciousness as the primary factor that determines the growth and development of humanity.

Let us return to the question of the human population in comparison with all other animals. The most important point is the fact that there are a hundred thousand times more of us than animals that are comparable to us based on diet and weight, such as wolves or bears at our latitude, or large monkeys in tropical countries (Figure 1). This essential fact demands an explanation. After all, these animals were regarded as our distant ancestors in the mythological consciousness of primeval people. However, between us and them there are no intermediate forms, which might in simple terms explain the creation and evolution of man; as if man falls outside the animal world. Ideas such as this serve to guide those who still insistently propose non-evolutionary paths for the emergence of intelligent man.

Biologically and by evolution man is very close to the animal kingdom. Nevertheless, there are no animals comparable to man either biologically or nutritionally; animal populations exist in a limited natural habitat, and the number of different species is determined by the dynamic equilibrium with the surrounding environment, which never developed as swiftly as that of man.

> *"It is our developed consciousness, language and culture that make us different from animals, and that is why there are a hundred thousand times more of us than there are animals comparable to us."*

The growth of our population is extremely unusual and is happening right before our eyes: 75 years ago I was taught at school that there were two billion people on Earth; at present there are almost seven billion of us. This singles us out amidst the entire animal world and makes our species, the growth of its populatio and its development, so distinctive. Furthermore, people living in the Neolithic Period, 10,000 years ago, surrounded themselves with domesticated animals, which also multiplied in quantities far surpassing their wild counterparts in headcount. Thus, the number of cattle in the world stands at more than two billion, and their emissions of gasses that affect the climate, such as methane and carbon dioxide, into the atmosphere are comparable in scale to emissions from human industrial activity. The aforementioned circumstances must be taken into account when we address the general problems of growth and the development of mankind.

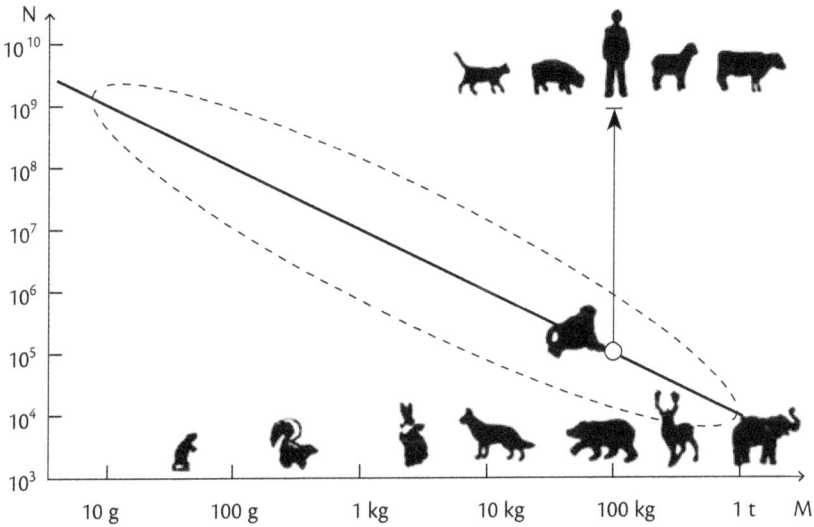

Figure 1. The numbers of various species of animal on Earth in relation to their mass

At the same time man represents one species – *Homo sapiens*—the intelligent human, with one uniform number of chromosomes, enabling people from different races to interbreed. But specifically in terms of intelligence, man differs from the entire animal kingdom, and it is because of his developed mind and language that mankind's population has grown so rapidly.

In order to present the various stages of growth and development over time, it would be useful to analyze this growth on different scales, regarding them as a *magnifying glass of time* (Compare Figures 2, 5, 7, 8, 9, 18 and Table 1).

N, millions

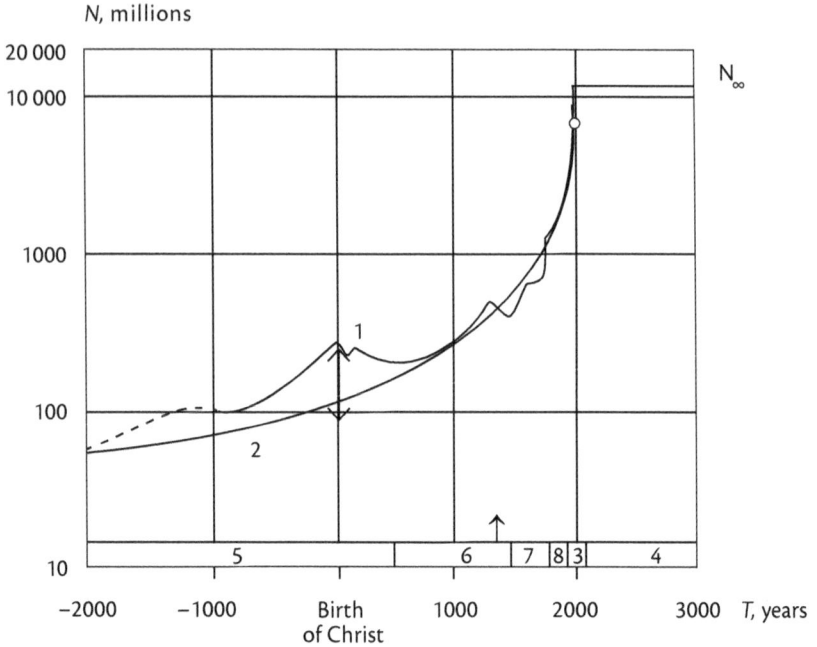

Figure 2. Population of the world from 2000 B.C. to 3000 A.D.

1 – population of the world from -2000 to our time; 2 – explosive
rate, leading to intensifying of the process of growth in the world's
population; 3 – demographic transition; 4 –stabilization of the
population; 5 – Ancient World; 6 – Middle Ages; 7 – Modern and 8 –
Recent history, ↑ – plague epidemic of 1348; ↕ – dispersion of data;
○ – N (1995) = 5.7 billion; N_∞ = 11.4 billion. If we were to imagine the
entire duration of the development of mankind in the time scale of
this graph from the time of anthropogenesis, then the period 5 million
years ago is located 50 meters to the left. This indicates how uneven the
passage of historical time is, as a consequence of which the duration of
historical eras decreases proportionately as we approach the moment
of demographic transition and stabilization of the world's population.

In conclusion, we note that besides the fundamental meaning of works
such as this in terms of understanding the development of humanity as
a whole, studies of global history of this kind are also necessary in order
to make sense of the fates that could await our country. Due to its geographical expanse, history and a variety of social and economic conditions,
Russia is a microcosm of these global processes. It is therefore essential for

us, taking into account the historic scale of these problems, to understand them on the level of all of humanity, and this provides an opportunity to address Russian problems in a critical epoch of global history in a new way.

Thus, a newly proposed vision of the past is based on a quantitative approach to anthropology and history. At the same time these representations touch upon fundamental global problems and economic issues, and criteria for the stability of development are related to questions of global safety. In particular, this opens the way to understanding the systemic socio-economic crisis which came so suddenly and is evolving so swiftly in the world.

Modeling Humanity's Global Growth

The answer to the central question—to what does man owe his development, the result of which is that there are five times as many of him as of all comparable animals—is associated with human consciousness by both anthropology and history.

However, for the author, the task consists of being able to express this conclusion in the language of physical theories and mathematical models, which are based on the fundamental concepts of society and humans which are accepted in the sciences.

For a description of the growth of humanity, three fundamental trajectories of development may be examined (Figure 3). The first shows the linear growth A, where the number of the population N is growing proportionally to time, T, and the speed of growth is constant. The graph of linear growth is best reflected on a linear grid for time and population numbers. During exponential growth, B, the speed of growth is already proportional to the population itself, and in this case the characteristic time for growth emerges. In mathematics it is acceptable to refer to time as T_E of exponential growth of the system in e, where $e = 2.72$ – the basis of natural logarithms. It is often referred to as a more visual time doubling, $T_2 = T_E \ln2 = 0.7\ T_E$, which is 30% less than T_E.

The exponential growth is reflected by a straight line on semi-logarithmic grid, on which time, T, is represented by a linear scale, and population N – by a logarithmic scale.

Here one sees how the human population has been growing over the past 4,000 years (Figure 2). This picture of humanity's development is presented on a semi-logarithmic grid, where the population for the past 4,000 years has increased one hundred times, puzzling demographers. If the population of the world has been growing exponentially, then, on such a grid, the growth would have been reflected as a straight line, which is not the case for humanity in either of the stages of growth, in the past nor in the present (Figure 3).

The growth of humanity happens in a completely different way. The graph in Figure 3 shows how at first slow growth accelerates, and as it approaches the third millennium, near the turn of the century, the population of the world suddenly rushes toward infinity in the demographic explosion, following the graph of hyperbola C.

This natural law of growth, for which there is no typical time of growth either, is of fundamental interest to us, since the data for the population of the world over a period of a million years is described by the formula below with remarkable accuracy:

$$N = \frac{200 \cdot 10^9}{2025 - T} = \frac{C}{T_1 - T}, \tag{1}$$

where $C = 200$ billion—a constant with dimension [human × years], and time is expressed in years.

It should be noted that the law of growth emerges as an obvious way to describe data about humanity's growth. Therefore, it is no surprise that many researchers discovered this natural law at various times. One of the first was the first British epidemiologist A. Mackendrick (1876–1943), as was pointed out to the author by Nathan Keyfitz, a leading American demographer. Later, in the 1960s, an American engineer, Forster, and a German physicist, Chorner, referred to this equation.

The latter examined the possibility of coping with infinitely expanding population numbers by spreading humans to other planets in our Solar System. I first met Chorner at the International Astronautics Congress in Dresden, where I gave a plenary speech on global problems and population growth, and he told me about his work and ideas. The Congress stuck strongly in my memory, since it took place at the time of the reunification of Germany in October of 1990.

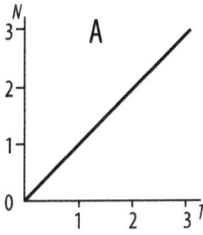

$$\frac{dN}{dT} = A, \quad N = AT \qquad \frac{d\ln N}{d\ln T} = 1$$

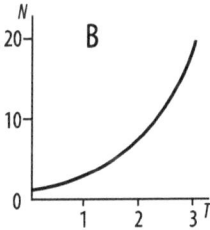

$$\frac{dN}{dT} = \frac{N}{T_E}, \quad N = N_0 \exp\frac{T}{T_E}$$

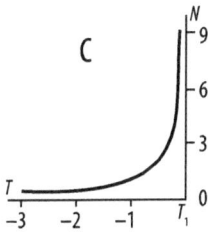

$$\frac{dN}{dT} = \frac{N^2}{C}, \quad N = \frac{C}{T_1 - T},$$

$$\frac{d\ln N}{d\ln T} = -1$$

Figure 3.

Linear growth – A, exponential growth – B, and hyperbolic growth – C

Finally, the Soviet astrophysicist I.S. Shklovsky referred to the rule stated above in the 6th, posthumous edition of a remarkable book, *Universe, Life, Intelligence* [13]. Relying on this model, he came to the conclusion that growth takes shape and limits itself based on social factors, rather than biological factors or factors related to resources.

On one hand, these works point to the contradictory nature of the model of limitless growth. On the other hand, in demography the expression (1), characterizing the hyperbolic growth of the population of the world, has never been taken seriously, for three reasons.

First of all, it was commonplace in demographics to look at the population of Earth simply as the sum of individual populations that were not interrelated. After all, the task of demography was seen as explaining growth in relation to specific social and economic conditions, which are impossible to formulate for the entire population of the world, and in particular to relate the speed of growth to the entire population of Earth.

Second of all, the expression (1) deals with infinity to the extent that we approach 2025, and does not have any significance beyond this date. Finally, this expression leads to problems estimating population size in the remote past. Thus, 20 billion years ago, when the Universe was born according to views of cosmology, there should already have been ten people in existence, who would no doubt have been cosmologists themselves, observing and discussing the birth of the Universe!

Nevertheless, the consistency of this law of growth over a broad range of time is striking, and if we were to proceed based on assessments of population in the past with which we are familiar, it holds true during an increase in the population by tens of thousands of times. It has thus described the development of humanity from the time of the appearance of *Homo habilis*—skilled man, 1.5 million years ago, but proper attention was not given to this.

The size of humanity at this moment is of great interest, and it was for that reason that I consulted a famous French anthropologist, a professor at the College de France, Yves Coppens, asking him: how many people lived at that time? His answer was succinct and precise—a hundred thousand, i.e. as many as there were large animals comparable to humans. This assessment is based on the observation that at that time, in South and East Africa, there were about a thousand large families, each containing around a hundred people.

This estimate does not contradict assessments by other authors relating to this important time in the history of humanity in the epoch of anthropogenesis, the first discoveries of which were made by the British anthropologist Leakey[6]. Thereafter, substantial contributions were made by a French expedition, led by Coppens, researching the early epoch of humanity's formation. Specifically in this epoch, the hyperbolic growth of our planet's population began, when its numbers increased proportionally to the square of the population of the world, right up to our time.

Therefore, when we refer to the development of the population as a single dynamic system, we will examine the equation (1) not only as a generalization of historical data, but also as an objective pattern and mathematically substantive expression. It characterizes the growth of the population as a self-similar process, developing along a hyperbolic trajectory, given that the function of growth (1) is a uniform function.

This property, which had been discovered earlier by Euler[7], points to the fact that there is no characteristic inner scale in such functions. Such a function is linear. However, exponential growth does not possess this quality, since it takes shape in the inner setting of exponential time, T_E. Uniform functions, linear or hyperbolic, describe the growth as a self-similar or self-stimulating process, in which relative growth is unchangeable at all times. Only at certain derived points—peculiarities or singularities—is this self-similarity disturbed.

In the case of growth along the hyperbola, this happens in the remote past, when the population asymptotically approaches zero, or at that critical moment, T_1, when N turns into infinity at the moment of intensification. In this singularity, under which the function (1) moves toward infinity, the main attraction of this formula is contained, since right then the fundamental change in the development of the system takes place, tied with demographic transition from swift growth to stability in the population of the world.

An exceptional role in the process of these studies was played by Sergei Pavlovich Kurdyumov[8]. The lecture about the growth of the Earth's population at his seminar was a breakthrough—a genuine revelation for me

---

[6] Mary Leakey was a British paleoanthropologist who discovered the first fossilized *Proconsul* skull, an extinct ape now believed to be ancestral to humans.

[7] pioneering Swiss mathematician and physicist

[8] A specialist in mathematical physics, mathematical modeling, plasma physics, complexity studies and synergetics from Moscow, Russia

and the team at the Keldysh Institute of Applied Mathematics[9]. The fact is that in contemporary applied mathematics, *processes with intensification* such as this, under which one or a few models of based values approach infinity over a finite span of time, are of great interest [16, 17].

This growth happens faster when there is intensification than when there is exponential growth—in this case, the time taken up by exponential growth itself becomes less and less dependent on the approach to a critical date, whereas under exponential growth the characteristic time is constant.

Kurdyumov and his colleagues developed powerful mathematical methods for a range of problems of regimes with intensification. This opened the possibility of grounds for the representation of synergy, developed by the German physicist Haken, for the description of the processes of development in complex systems [18]. These methods found application in the theory of explosive processes, shock waves, in the physics of phase transformations, and also in the description of irregular processes in systems' development in chemical kinetics and laser theory. Now these views of non-linear problems in the physics of complex systems have found application for humanity as a whole, having become the basis for new quantitative results and instructive qualitative analogies.

Before turning to the conclusions that stem from the law of hyperbolic growth, it is necessary to define the meaning of the constant value of C, which determines the population of Earth one year before particularity. Thus, this constant depends on the chosen unit of time, and the year, founded on the time taken by the Earth to orbit the Sun, but does not express the nature of humanity. However, if one's own unit of time, determined by the practical duration of human life, is inserted, then this opens a path toward defining the borders of the application of a simple law of growth (1).

This time, $\tau = 45$ years is close to the average age of the world's population, and in the limits of the model, it appears as a semi sphere of global demographical transition (Figure 5). Then, under the construction of the model, time should be expressed on the scale of $\tau = 45$ years and instead of dimensional constant, C, it would make sense to insert the constant K:

---

[9] The research institute specializing in computational mathematics

$$K = \sqrt{C/\tau} = 60\ 000.$$

This large parameter is a dimensionless number and defines all the correlations which emerge under the formation of the theory of growth. Later on, in all deductions of this theory, this number becomes the main characteristic—the parameter for order in that dynamic system, the development of which we are examining.

Thus, the number $K \sim 100000$ is determined as the initial population of *Homo* 1.6 million years ago and the limit, toward which the population of Earth is moving, $\sim K^2 \approx 10$ billion, and the continuation of humanity's development turns out to be about $T_0 \approx K\tau \sim 3$ billion years. The magnitude of the order K determines the scale of a self-sufficient population, such as a university city, a science town or part of a megalopolis, such as Moscow with its population of ~10 million, divided between ~ 100 districts with ~ 100,000 people in each. When we analyze these fluctuations, it turns out that K determines the primary scale of correlation between population and the number of structures when humanity organizes itself. For instance, nations with a population of fewer than 50,000 are generally considered to have low populations.

The fundamental quality of hyperbolic explosive development is that the speed of growth is proportional not to the initial quantity of the population, as in exponential growth, reflecting mankind's ability to multiply, but the second degree—the square of the quantity of the population of the world. This points to a significant degree of regularity, which should be interpreted as cooperative growth, described by quadratic interaction, proportional to $\sim N^2$.

The change of the indicator of a degree from the unit for exponential growth to two for hyperbolic growth, leads to a new character in the growth and development of humanity. This is no affine-tuning of a model that was accepted earlier, but the emergence of a qualitatively new pattern in the description of the growth of the population—in our case, the growth of all of humanity.

However, this pattern cannot be identified with an interaction between a man and a woman, because we are dealing with all the connections, encompassing all the processes of interaction in the world's population system.

Thus genuine research is devoted to the study of all the consequences of this interaction, which is analogous to the interaction of Van der Waals[10] in non-ideal gas. It has been studied in depth in molecular physics and also in physics systems that consist of various particles. The processes that depend on the square of the number of the particles arise with a description of chemical reactions of the second order in chemical kinetics. These processes can be described as a ramified chain reaction which asymptotically leads to square dependency between the speed of reaction and time, which was pointed out to the author by G.B. Manelis[11]. As an example of such processes involving intensification, we could consider the atomic bomb, where the result of branched chain reactions happens to be a nuclear explosion.

The quadratic growth of our planet's population points to an analogous, much slower, but no less dramatic process, when generalized information is the result of a chain reaction, and multiplies with every stage of growth, thus identifying the increasing rates of a population's development throughout the entire world. In such systems, with strong connection between the particles, as a result of self-organization, collective degrees of freedom arise. The growth of the world's population is described by the equation:

$$\frac{dN}{dt} = \frac{N^2}{K^2},\qquad(2)$$

where time $dt = dT/\tau$ is measured in units $\tau = 45$ years.

In this nonlinear differential equation of growth, development is expressed through the square of the total number of people on Earth at the current moment in time, attributed to the square of the constant, K. This equation for growth is the basis of all the views that have been formulated with regard to the collective interaction and the conclusions that stem from it. According to this developed understanding, the growth of humanity occurs as a result of the cooperative mechanism of the

---

[10] Also known as Van der Waals force, named after Dutch scientist Johannes Diderik van der Waals, is the sum of the attractive or repulsive forces between molecules

[11] A Russian physicist who specialized in the field of technical chemistry and chemical physics

multiplying of our numbers. The causes for this can vary, although as we shall see, the collective mechanism makes them an effective means for describing growth on the scale of the whole of humanity.

Since we are looking at a phenomenological description of growth, the specific interpretation of the facts of growth yields to the overall qualities of the evolutionary systems developed in theoretical physics. However, the model for self-similar growth, following the formula (2), has limited the field of application in time, partially due to the fact that this expression is asymptotic.

In physics, asymptotic approximation is understood to mean the possibility of disregarding the processes, not showing in this the approach of any substantial impact [14, 15]. This reception is widely used in physics, since it is often possible to assess which processes could be neglected based on qualitative reasoning, and thereby construct an approximate theory. Moreover, in physics, nearly all theories have this character, and therein lies the stark difference between physics and mathematics.

Imagine a conversation like this taking place between a physicist and a mathematician:

Physicist: If $5 \times 5 = 25$ and $6 \times 6 = 36$, then consequently, $7 \times 7 = 47$!

Mathematician: This is monstrous and totally incorrect, since it can be proven beyond doubt that $7 \times 7 = 49$.

Physicist: Perhaps that is so. But $7 \times 7 = 47$ is almost correct, and for our purposes it will do nicely!

This is an exaggeration, of course, but at the heart of the approximate asymptotic methods, developed in order to examine complex systems in cooperation, lies the calculation of the distinctions between processes of growth in various time scales.

"At the heart of approximate asymptotic methods lies the calculation of the distinctions between processes of growth in various time scales."

When applied to humanity, this means that a slow, century-long global development, comparable with one's own scale of time with moving into the past, should be differentiated from fast processes related to specific historical events. These processes are limited in time and space and occur on a scale commensurate with human life over a typical time frame of ~ 45 years. In historical sciences, Fernand Braudel[12] pointed to this influence of time scale: "Historians have recently started to single out this distinction in the form of temporary structures and connections. The first scale refers to long-term exigencies, the second to short-term ones." [6]

Rapid processes are chaotic and are determined by accidental factors, which lead to the stochastics of a particular history. These processes, with their descriptions, demand reference to the theory of accidental processes. On the other hand, a century-long process of growth is self-similar and determined. In other words, on all levels of the auto-model process, its nature does not change and the average relative speed of growth remains unchanging. It makes sense to look at the logarithmic speed of growth, which is better seen on a graph built on a double logarithmic grid, where time and population numbers are represented by logarithms (Figure 9).

On this graph, it can be clearly seen how the change of regimes of self-similar growth occurs and how the specialty of growth in the beginning of anthropogenesis with T_0 = 5–4 million years is overcome. When linear growth began with one person and ended with the peculiarity of growth at passing of the pole at T_1 = 1995. Close to this peculiarity of growth is the vicinity of the pole, and in the jargon of mathematicians, it is beaten out.

Thus, the growth defines systematic development, where the driving factor of the auto-model growth turns out to be the connections between the global network community, encompassing the whole of humanity in an effective informational field. Scaling, or self-similarity, of growth presents an essential understanding in dynamic development. In the case of processes that take place in time, this means overall constancy—invariance of the nature of the movement. We will explain the aforementioned statements with examples, taken for the sake of clarity from the field of mechanics.

An important and extremely simple example is movement by inertia. It was Galileo who came to the realization that a material body, free from the influence of external forces, moves by inertia at a constant speed. He

---

[12] A French historian and a leader of the Annales School. His scholarship focused on three main projects, each representing several decades of intense study: *The Mediterranean* (1923–49, then 1949–66), *Civilization and Capitalism* (1955–79), and the unfinished *Identity of France* (1970–85).

showed that such movement is self-similar—at all moments in time the movement occurs in the same way, and only via the application of external forces can this movement be altered.

Self-similar movement such as this occurs when a constant external power acts on it, such as the force of gravity on a falling body, or the force of a rope's pull, while holding a stone moving in a circle—movements such as this are self-similar, too. However, if the rope were to snap suddenly, the stone would fly off instinctively in a straight line. The effect of a sling is based on this principal, when one type of movement is replaced by another, is also self-similar. It is important to keep in mind that the regimes stated are realized over a long period, and changes to them can take place almost instantaneously. In essence, such processes are observed within the growth of the scale of humanity's development, which is why such examples are helpful in illustrating the role of differences in times within the development of the system.

Taking the differences in time and speed relative to growth into account, this gives us the key to understanding the fundamental character of the informational mechanism in the development of humanity. This is why, when referring to views of physics and the language of mathematics, it is important to bring these views into line with the images and concepts of historians and economists, such that in interdisciplinary collaboration, their views can be related to the concepts that lie at the heart of the model. This enabled a new understanding of the many quantitative peculiarities of the global history of humanity. The instant significance of exponential growth in the past can be determined by such a path. Calculations show that characteristic time is equal to the age of the event, starting from the moment of demographic transition—1995.

The interpretation of such development has led to the fundamental assumption that collective cooperation is determined by the mechanism of expansion and the reproduction of generalized information on the scale of humanity, driving its development. Thereby, the origin and nature of the quadratic law of the growth of humanity should be united by the transmission and duplication of information. Thus, relying on the principals of physics, for the first time in elementary expressions, it has been possible to describe the dynamic development of humanity over more than a million years—from the first appearance of mankind, gifted with consciousness, to the beginning of demographic transition and beyond, into the foreseeable future.

After the main singularity—the divergence at T_1 at the time of demographic transition, there is a decrease in the speed of growth to zero. After this, the asymptotic stabilization of the population of the world follows, reaching the point 11.4 billion; equal to a doubling of the population at the moment of transition in 1995. This scenario of development corresponds to the same one that demographers arrived at independently from an analysis of observations and intuitive understandings (Figure 8).

The question of the stability of hyperbolic growth is pertinent. According to conclusions of synergy, as a result of non-linear connection, rapid internal processes stabilize the century-long hyperbolic development of the population of the world close to the demographic revolution itself, when growth can no longer keep up with development. Therefore, specific historical processes that are of a localized or chaotic character stabilize global development. The evidence of ancient stability can be observed in the regularity of the historical period of growth.

To help explain the aforementioned concepts, there are mechanical equivalents. Similarly, the stability of a whirligig in space is due to the effect of hyperbolic forces acting upon it while it is spinning. These forces, when the spindle of the whirligig is disturbed, result in slow processional movement near the location of dynamic equilibrium. A pendulum with fast fluctuations of its pendant acts in a similar way, stabilizing the slow movement of the pendulum itself near the position of equilibrium.

Similar examples of behavior in larger systems help us understand the development of a system as complex as humanity, where the population of the Earth on average persistently follows a statistically determined path of self-similar growth, managed by the interior dynamic of growth and stabilized by the chaos of local history. This is why the chaotic nature of history makes the creation of a determinative theory of history, which is limited in time and space, difficult [48, 49].

Thus, the growth and development of humanity is obliged to human consciousness, its culture and developed system for the transmission of knowledge vertically, from generation to generation, as well as horizontally along the space of our planet, which manages this global process, no matter how specific the mechanism of growth is. If the scholar singles out a human from other types of animals comparable to himself, then it is specifically in the development of consciousness that further research should take place as we look for answers to human evolution and the riddle of the immense speed of the growth of humanity, as the population is connected through information.

Recent research offers explanations for the appearance of mechanisms of growth, constructed using the methods of molecular biology. They showed that a critical event seems to have been the mutation of one or two genes of HAR1 F, which define the way the brain is arranged in the 5th-9th weeks of the embryo's development. The leader of an international project, Kathrin Pollard, reported on this research in an article entitled *What Makes Us Human?* [19]. Note, however, that these results still require proof, of which none exists at the time of writing. Nonetheless, there is currently every reason to believe that an unexpected change such as this to the genome of our ancestors 5–4 million years ago could have led to a qualitative leap in the way the brain is organized. This was the reason for the development of social consciousness and culture, which led to an extraordinary quantitative growth in humanity.

As a result of this mutation, speech and language appeared, as well as the mastery of fire and stone tools after a prolonged era of anthropogenesis. Since that time the biological nature of man has changed little despite the swift process of our social development. This is why the understanding of the latter is so significant today, when it turned out that non-linear evolution of the population growth of humanity, founded on the informational collective mechanism of growth and obeying one's own inward forces, determines not only the explosive development, but also its limit.

This leads to an understanding of the phenomenological principle of the *demographic imperative*, which maintains that growth is initially defined by the inward processes of humanity's development and not by resources or special factors such as migration. This is different than the demographic imperative derived from Malthus' population principal, according to which the growth of the population is limited by outside resources. Furthermore, we can come to the conclusion that "substantial economic and political conclusions consist in the fact that the struggle for the resources that secure growth cannot be viewed as a factor which determines global development."

This substantial affirmation must be understood correctly, since it has far-reaching effects in terms of detecting the paths of development open to humanity in the foreseeable future, when it is not collective growth, but the development of quality that will be the central factor in our social evolution. Indeed, contemporary historical experience in developed areas, primarily the USA, Northern Europe and Japan, suggests that this conclusion is well-founded.

Thus growth proportional to the number of humans squared, is not determined through the development of independent units or even groups of people, but depends on the collective interaction of all of humanity. In the context of such an approach, growth is viewed as the non-local interaction of all of humanity, evolving and developing as a whole—as a super organism. These presentations resonate with V.I. Vernadsky's[13] idea about the noosphere and found expression in the concepts of a contemporary society of knowledge, as set out in the Universal presentation by UNESCO [31].

These concepts can be connected to the concept of the anthroposphere, and the system of spreading and developing knowledge is realized by means of what I.P. Pavlov[14] referred to as the second signal system. This concept, put forth in 1932, states that the conditioned reflex is inherent to the human system, and it is this which defines the principal difference in the workings of the brains of animals and of humans.

The second signal system functions at the highest levels of the central nervous system, and builds on the principles of the first signal system, becoming active first and foremost in speech stimulators. Whereas the brain of an animal responds only to direct visual, auditory, or other stimuli or traces of them, when the sensations aroused compose an image of reality, the human possesses, in addition to this, the ability to find a generalized expression, using words, for countless signals from the first signal system.

---

[13] He was a Russian and Soviet mineralogist and geochemist who is considered one of the founders of geochemistry, biogeochemistry, and of radiogeology. His ideas of noosphere were an important contribution to Russian cosmism

[14] He was a famous Russian physiologist

Moreover, the word, as Pavlov expressed it, becomes the signal of all signals at the transition from words to language.

The first and second signal systems are essentially different levels of a single higher nervous activity. However, in human nature, the second signal system plays the leading role. Analysis and synthesis, which are carried out by the cortex of the large hemispheres of the brain, are linked already not so much with specific independent irritants, but with the generalized forms of them as well, as presented in images and concepts, and expressed in words. This is all thanks to the presence of the second signal system. The function of abstract reflection on occurrences and objects provided humans with unlimited possibilities to orient themselves in the world around them, and ultimately allowed them to create science.

The formation of the second signal system takes place only under the influence of interaction between a human being and other people. In other words, it is determined by the upbringing and education received in society. Therefore, in order to achieve fully-fledged development of personality, the timely and correct development of both signal systems is necessary.

A paradoxical feature of many social sciences was the emphasis on distinctions in culture, traditions and religious views. However, a fundamental study of human nature points to the deep unity of humanity as a system, in which unique qualities, which can be attributed to the phenomena of our mind, are realized. Interdisciplinary studies of the nature of humanity as a whole are therefore important. Furthermore, it is difficult to conclude that problems such as this can be solved by reducing them to the sum of the private contributions made by separate and distinct ideas of several experts, living and working in their intellectual and methodological enclaves.

Therefore, the informational unity of humanity is essential in the development of Earth's population as a system. In the past, the connecting role between East and West on the Eurasian supercontinent was performed by trading systems such as the Silk Road[15].

This convoy network with various branches helped spread not just merchandise but also knowledge, ideas, customs and religious views as well.

---

[15] The Silk Road or Silk Route is a historical network of interlinking trade routes across the Afro-Eurasian landmass that connected East, South, and Western Asia with the Mediterranean and European world, as well as parts of North and East Africa

Buddhism came into Central Asia from India through the Khyber Pass[16], and spread to the West towards Kalmykia[17] and to the East by the North pass into Mongolia, China and Japan. Other networks of caravan paths bound the countries and cultures of Africa and Europe.

Thus, in the ancient past, processes of the exchange and interpenetration of cultures, a considerable role was played by the migration of people, occurring under the influence of climate change. The informational unity of humanity developed from this very deep antiquity and is expressed in a dual influence of cultures. Shamanism, which sprang into existence no less than a hundred thousand years ago, points to a mutual root of this global occurrence, relics of which have lasted until our time. Linguists, from their point of view, came to this conclusion about the underlying structural unity of the languages of the world.

The Demographic Revolution

To understand humanity's development, one may first observe the limits of a regime's domain of self-similar growth, narrowed by two main features. First of all, in the ancient past the growth is found to be too slow. Therefore, to exclude this peculiarity of growth from consideration, when time becomes infinitely long, and the population strives toward zero slower and slower, it is necessary to speculate that in the epoch of anthropogenesis, the minimal speed of growth cannot be less than the emergence of one hominid over a characteristic time of continuation of a generation.

This simple hypothesis is enough to insert the minimal speed of growth and describe the processes of anthropogenesis as a linear growth of the population of people gifted by intellect. Even such a naïve hypothesis turns out to be effective and leads to a reasonable evaluation of the duration of the era that is distant from us. Furthermore, it is revealed that we could

---

[16] The Khyber Pass is a mountain pass connecting Afghanistan and Pakistan, cutting through the northeastern part of the Spin Ghar mountains

[17] The Republic of Kamykia is a federal subject of Russia and is the only Buddhist region in Europe

accept the microscopic time that is equal to = 45 years, which is identical in the past as well as in the present, and points to consistency of this constant, defined by the biological nature of humanity from the time of his appearance.

In the examination of the critical moment of the year 2000 which marks the peak of demographic explosion and the era of demographical transition itself, the speed of growth must be limited from the above by the natural limits doubling over time of the sequence = 45 years as a measure of effective reproductive human life. Due to the impossibility of the further continuation of self-similar growth during demographic explosion, the **regime with intensification** advances and growth concludes with the demographic transition with a sharp change of all processes of our development.

Therefore, demographic transition leads to a change in the rate of growth and the stabilization of the population [21]. This major occurrence in the development of the population of a country was discovered by a French demographer, Adolf Landry, using the example of France (Figure 4).

In the 18th century, France lived through not only its Great Political Revolution, which took place in 1789, but also its demographic revolution. Political revolution is marked by such notable events as the Storming of the Bastille or the destruction of privileges; in a span of a few years, much was irreversibly changed and was replaced by the existing order.

But there was nothing as sensational that would have marked that the approach of another revolution had begun. Its development was unnoticeable and relatively slow. Nevertheless, in no small degree, it is a revolution, so far as when the regime changes, a revolution occurs. This holds true in demography just as it does in any other field. Suddenness of change does not appear necessary. Indeed, talking about demographic revolution, under which the change of unlimited to limited reproduction takes place, there is every ground to keep to the given definition without any other additions.

The global demographic transition lies in the change from a time of growth to a period in which the world's population is stable.

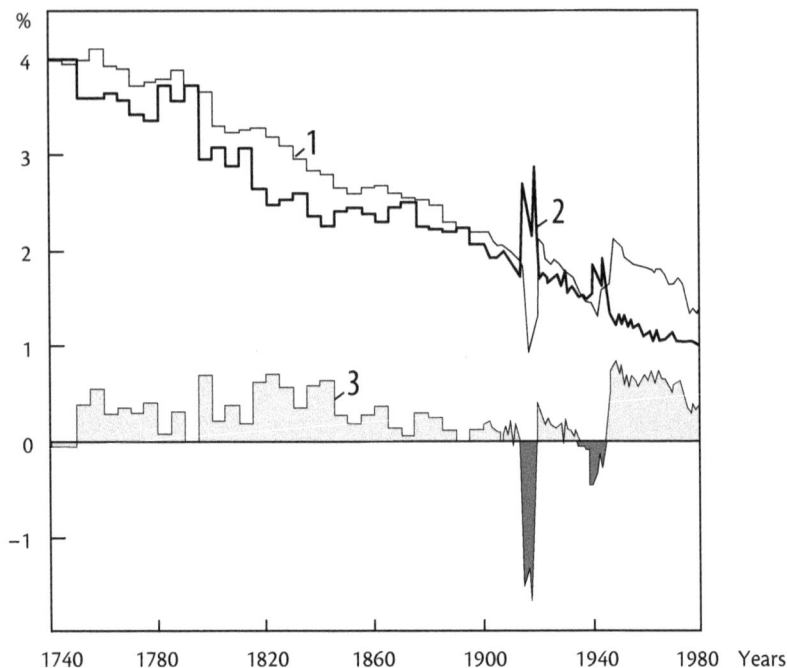

Figure 4. Population trends and demographic transition in France [21]

1 – birth rate, 2 – death rate and 3 – population growth rate (% per year, averaged over the decade).

If demographers have researched this phenomenon on the scale of the country and defined it as a transition, then we will think of the transition as a global event and, following Landry, a **global demographic revolution.** For the population of the world, the transition is shown in Figure 5, and for individual countries in Figure 6. In these figures it is evident that an aggregate global demographic transition is occurring almost simultaneously all over the world, despite the differing histories and economies of the countries of which humanity consists. Indeed, the transition in the so-called developed countries is unfolding somewhat more slowly and is only 50 years ahead of the transition for the entire population of Earth. This synchronicity and the effective narrowing of the transition, which undoubtedly intensified in the period of demographic

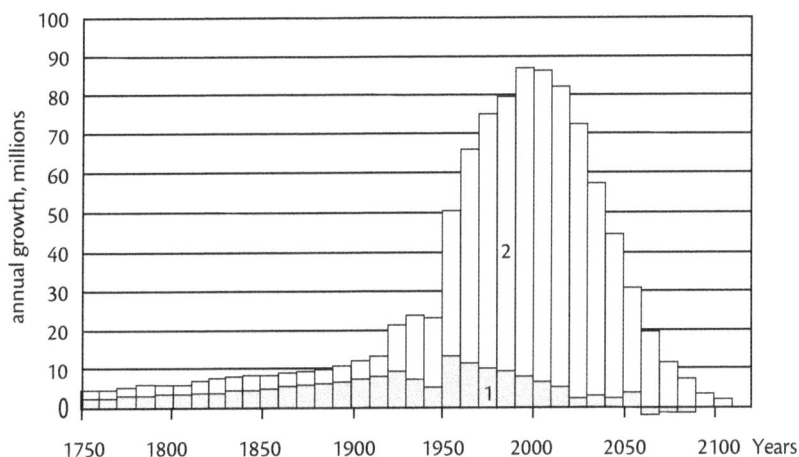

Figure 5. Global demographic transition, 1750–2100.

Annual increase averaged over decades. The decrease in the rate of growth during the world wars and the demographic echo of war at the beginning of the 21th century is seen on the graph in 1 – developed and 2 - developing countries (data from the UN).

revolution, amount to strong evidence of global unity in the processes of growth and the systemic nature of the Earth's population.

This provides a basis for the explanation and understanding of the process of globalization, which is attracting so much attention from contemporary academics at the moment because it is taking place at a time close to τ [51]. However, in the past, including the most distant period at the dawn of humanity, we already started developing as a global system. Only the rate of development of globalization was as slow as the growth of the population, for which typical time equals the age of the era.

The discourse is therefore about a single approach to gaining an understanding of the entire passage of the global history of humanity, unchangeable over the course of 1.6 million years—from the emergence of *Homo habilis* to the modern crisis in its development.

Until the demographic transition itself, this growth was dynamically self-similar and ran such that the relative—logarithmic—speed of growth was constant and the average development of the entire human population—the whole of humanity—was characterized by this.

"The demographic revolution and transition to the constant population is, undoubtedly, the largest event in the development of humanity through the whole of history."

Moreover, the changes will affect all aspects of our lives, and we, as accident would have it, have become witnesses to this grand revolution in humanity's history. A comprehensive analysis of this phenomenon must therefore be at the center of our attention. It must also be taken into consideration during the analysis of all aspects of humanity's growth. None of the events of the past—neither wars nor epidemics, nor even climate change, are incommensurable with the events unfolding at the present time. These events are directly related to ideas about the role of the mind and consciousness of man, and culture, which lie at the heart of the theory of growth, as models for the collective behavior of the system of the Earth's population.

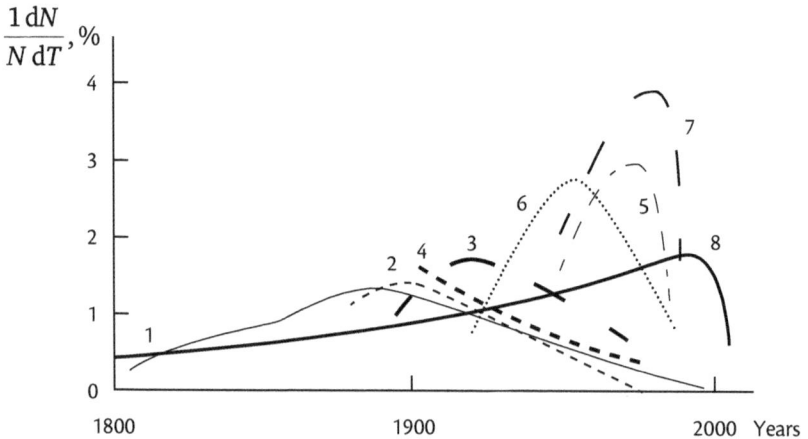

Figure 6. Demographic transition in various countries

The graphs are smoothed over and growth is stated in percentages per year. 1 – Sweden, 2 – Germany, 3 – USSR, 4 – USA, 5 – Mauritius, 6 – Sri Lanka, 7 – Costa Rica and 8 – the world in general. The formation of global transition can be seen in this graph. Whilst the transition in Sweden and France took 160 years, then the later it begins, the more rapidly it takes place.

In conclusion, the above-mentioned description of the global history of humanity enables us to break it into three epochs. The first epoch, **A,** is an epoch of anthropogenesis lasting 4–5 million years, which led to the appearance of an initial population of *Homo habilis* numbering about a hundred thousand ~ K. After this, epoch **B** begins—a period of explosive development along a hyperbolic trajectory. As the result of this, thanks to quadratic growth the limit ~ K^2 is reached, and humanity at this time settles all over the planet. It is notable that by this epoch of the Stone Age, humanity had lived through nine ice ages.

The Growth of World Population

The above picture of growth makes it possible to examine the entire development of humanity in general. The hyperbolic growth of humanity, occurring in the regime with intensification and surpassing all comparable processes in tens of thousands of times, becomes a dominant function in the solution of the differential equation of growth (2). The investment of the other processes that accompany growth is negligibly small and in the first approximation does not influence growth.

This epoch of quadratic growth is limited by two main features. The first lies in the distant past, when the quantity of people was small, and the period of growth was long. The second main feature is the global demographic revolution, when the time of transition is pushed down to the limit, and the population grows rapidly.

For each of these epochs growth is described asymptotically: it is linear at the beginning, hyperbolic in the flow of epoch B and constant at the exit from demographic transition. Upon the completion of the demographic revolution in epoch C, the population of Earth will reach ~ 11 billion, when the stabilization of the population of our planet should be expected. Naturally, this global schedule only describes the basic features of the growth of humanity, which, nevertheless, give a complete and acceptable picture of our growth and development as a global process.

It is important to note that the picture presented does not reflect the processes which are bound to trends in the movement of people, resources and everything that is related to economics and the system by which mankind sustains itself. The absence of these things in the model demands explanation, as many authors have considered these factors to be the specific bases for determining the growth and development of humanity. But under the regime with intensification, the special distribution of the population and everything related to specific social and economic conditions cannot dramatically influence growth when global explosive development is the all-prevailing force. Exceptional growth in the number of people explains why a simple asymptotic model of the regime with intensification proves to be so effective, to the extent that it describes the fundamental process of growth.

If we turn to the trend for the growth of humanity, then we will see that economics essentially appears to be something that is derived from growth and development, which are systematically bound to one another, rather than the cause of them. For this reason, special and economically significant variables and resources should not be factored in; by the first approximation it is not these factors that determine growth.

Also, in light of this, population migration should not be taken into account either, since this is an internal process flowing within the global system, and in the first approximation it does not alter the total number of people on the planet. Obviously, this is the case only when we examine the growth of all humanity and not just that of an individual country or even a whole region. Thus economics is subordinate to development, and not vice versa. Therein lies the solution to the paradox that rate of growth is not directly related to resources, and the system of life support is such that despite all the costs, humanity is developing by its own self-modeled path.

This is solved, in theory, by reference to the phenomenological approach. On the one hand, we are describing the behavior of the system as a whole: we are looking for the mechanisms of growth, not the causes of it. Moreover, there could be various reasons and the informational nature is one of them. On the other hand, searching for an explanation in detailed processes is extremely difficult, and is not necessary, inasmuch as we are dealing with a very connected system. It has powerful factors of its own within it, providing stable global growth and self-organization in spatial and temporal structures. For that reason, linear causative ties are not only unnecessary, but are also not applicable in principal.

"We are describing the behavior of the system as a whole: we are looking for the mechanisms of growth, not the causes of it."

The image of growth set out above gives us the opportunity to examine the entire development of humanity in detail and to sequentially study the demographic history of humanity as a whole, by developing a global phenomenological approach. This leads to an understanding of the statistical nature of the behavior of this difficult and unbalanced system, in which quantity determines the strength of the interrelationship within the system. Furthermore, we will later see that the internal time of growth is itself subordinate to the development of the system. In other words, global growth was determined by self-consistent and self-similar social systemic development, obliged to collective cooperation enveloping all of humanity. It is synchronizing development, and throughout the one million years of epoch B, the nature of this interaction remained virtually unchanged.

Fernand Braudel, in his monograph *Capitalism and Material Development 1400–1800*, after examining the development of humanity as a whole, notes that in global history,

> ...such prolonged correlations are observed beyond the limits of Europe as well. Roughly at the same time, China and India most likely progressed, developed and regressed to the same rhythm as the West, as if the entire global population was in the grip of a primary cosmic force, predetermining its fate. In comparison to this, the rest of history seems of secondary importance. The economist and demographer, Ernst Wagemann[18], adheres to the same view.
>
> This synchronicity is apparent in the 18th century, more than likely to have been present in the 16th century, and it is fair to assume that it was present in the 13th century—from France under Saint Louis[19] to the distant Mongol empire in China. It was as if this 'mixed' issues together and at the same time simplified them. Wagemann concludes that the growth of the population should have been ascribed to the effect of reasons utterly

---

[18] Ernst Wagemann was a German economist and demographer.

[19] Also known as Louis IX was King of France from 1226 until his death in 1270. He was the son of Louis VII and Blanche of Castile.

distinct from those which determine economic and technical progress and successes in medicine.

In any case, these fluctuations, which were synchronized to a greater or lesser extent from one end of earth's dry lands to the other, help us imagine and understand that different human masses over the centuries have found themselves to be in relatively stable collective correlation: one is equal to another, or is double the size of a third. If we know how big one of them is, we can calculate the size of the other and, by this means, generate (with the margin for error inherent in such a method of computation) a figure for the entire human population.

This global number is of interest for obvious reasons: no matter how indefinite and inexact it is, it will by necessity help us to portray the biological development of mankind, viewed as a single mass, as a single capital, as statisticians would have put it.

What is striking about this insightful testimony by a great historian is his clarity of understanding of the systemic essence of humanity's history, which lies at the foundation of the entire concept we have developed.

Table 1 contains a summary of the latest data about the population of Earth, from the emergence of humanity to the foreseeable future [23]. Throughout this entire period of population growth, the estimates of paleodemography are in accordance with the results of modeled calculations of population size. It is notable that the accuracy of the data about the recent past for the population of the world barely reaches 10%, and for the distant past ~100% from N. In particular, estimates of the population of the world at the beginning of our era differ by 2–3 times, as, for example, in the case of the interpretation of the size of the Chinese population during the flourishing of the Qin[20] and Han[21] Dynasties. But since we are talking about changes to the world's population by a factor of

---

[20] The Qin Dynasty was the first imperial dynasty of China, lasting from 221 to 206 BC. The dynasty was formed after the conquest of the six other states by the state of Qin, and its founding emperor was known as Qin Shi Huang, the First Emperor of Qin.

[21] The Han Dynasty was an imperial dynasty of China, preceded by the Qin Dynasty and succeeded by the Three Kingdoms. It was founded by the rebel leader Liu Bang, known posthumously as Emperor Gaozu of Han.

tens of thousands, such logarithmic precision proves sufficient and, on the whole, confirms the calculations.

The transitions, depending on τ, are shown in Figure 7. In the context of this growth model, the duration of the transition is determined by one time, equal to $\tau = 45$ years, and the choice of value is determined by the half-width of the global demographic transition, shown in Figure 9 and independently matching the size of the world's population in 1995.

Table 1. Growth of the population of Earth (millions)

Year	Population N	Model N_m	Year	Population N	Model N_m
-4.4×10^6	(0)	0	1960	3039	3245
-1.6×10^6	0.1	0.1	1965	3345	3497
-35000	1–5	2	1970	3707	3778
-15000	3–10	8	1975	4086	4089
-7000	10–15	16	1980	4454	4430
-2000	47	42	1985	4851	4801
0	100–230	86	1990	5277	5198
1000	275–345	173	**1995**	**5682**	**5613**
1500	440–540	345	2000	6073	6038
1650	465–550	492	2005	6453	6463
1750	735–805	685	2010	6832	6878
1800	835–907	851	2025	7896	7987
1850	1090–1110	1120	2050	9298	9259
1900	1608–1710	1625	2075	9879	9999
1920	1811	1970	2100	10400	10451
1930	2020	2196	2125	10700	10745
1940	2295	2474	2150	10800	10956
1950	2556	2817	2200	11000	11225
1955	2780	3019	2500	----	11364

"The more distant we are from the time examined, the lower the degree of precision of estimates, hence why we can refer only to orders of magnitude."

N, billions

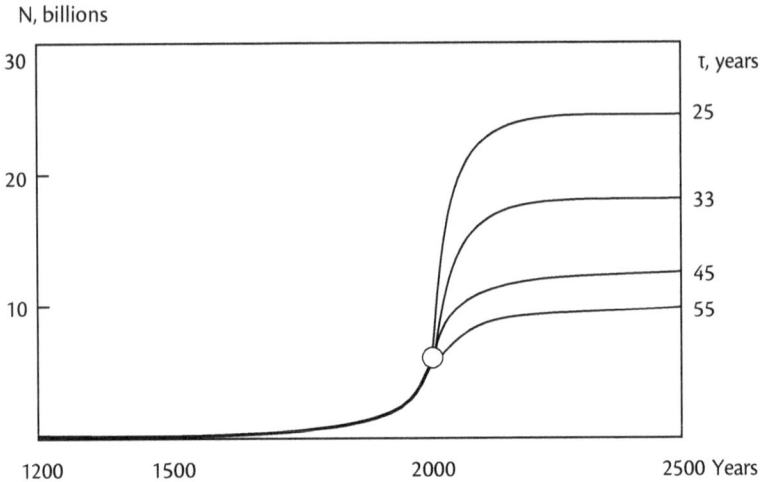

**Figure 7. Demographic transition of the population of the world
in relation to the characteristic of time τ**

Thus the value of distinctive time τ is determined by a range of factors in accordance with the independent characteristics of the entire system of the population of the world. In order to describe demographic transition, Chene inserted the demographic multiplier M, which indicates the extent to which population increases in the world as a result of demographic transition [21]. The duration of the transition amounts to $2\tau = 90$ years from its beginning at the moment in time $T_1 - \tau = 1950$ until its end, when $T_1 + \tau = 2040$. In the model M = 3.00, and the actual value of M = 2.95 and doesn't depend on the size of typical time (Figure 8).

These results also confirm the global nature of the demographic revolution; primarily the fact that the whole of humanity can be described as one whole, interconnected evolving system. For estimates of the population of the Earth in the foreseeable future, the results of the simulation should be compared to the calculations made by the International Institute of Applied System Analysis (IIASA), the UN and other agencies. The UN's forecast for 2150 is based on a series of scenarios for the birth rate and death rate across 9 regions of the world. In the best-case scenario, the population of Earth at this time will reach a constant

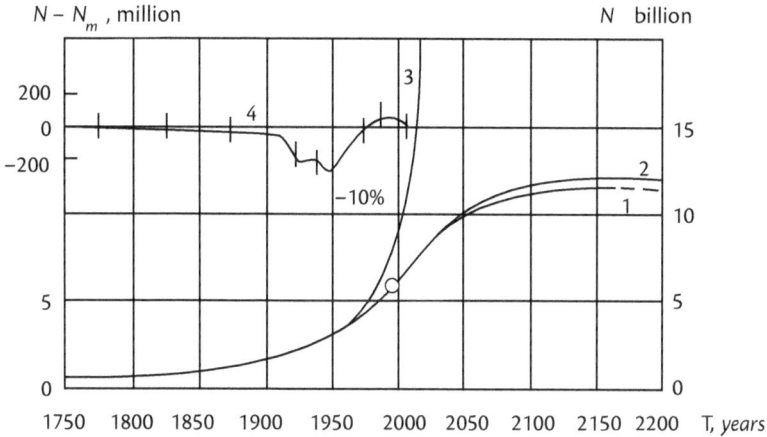

Figure 8. Growth in the world's population over the course of the demographic revolution, 1750–2200

1 – forecast of IIASA; 2 – model; 3 – explosive departure to infinity (regime with intensification); 4 – difference between estimate and population of the world , multiplied by a factor of 5, showing the total losses caused by the world wars in the 20th century; o – 1995. The duration of demographic transition amounts to $2\tau = 90$ years. The graph is shown in the linear view T and N.

limit of 11.6 billion people. Under the median scenario put forward by the UN's Department of Population for the year 2300, the population is expected to be at 9 billion people. Thus the forecasts of demographers and the theory of growth both lead us to conclude that the Earth's population is going to stabilize at the level of 9–11 billion and will not even be double the current figure.

Indeed, until the year 2000, the population of our planet grew at a constantly accelerating pace. Then, it seemed to many that the demographic explosion, overpopulation and the inevitable depletion of natural resources would lead to catastrophe. However, in 1995, when the population of the world reached 5.7 billion and the rate of population growth attained its peak value of 84 million people per year, which is equal to 220–240 thousand a day, or 10 thousand an hour - the rate of growth began to slow down, and this points to the start of the final phase of global demographic transition and foreseeable stabilization of the Earth's population.

Data on population growth and the function of growth enable us to determine the total number of people, $P_{0.1}$, who have at some point lived on Earth, from the moment of the beginning of anthropogenesis until the demographic revolution. This figure is equal to $P_{0.1} = 96$ billion, which accords closely with the recent assessment $P_{0.1} = 106$ billion made by Haub [24], and the calculations of other authors.

Our calculations point to the fact that in the entire history of mankind there have been $1 + lnK = 12$ cycles epochs of development and that there were $\Delta P = 2.25K^2 = 8$ billion people alive in each of them. Clearly, this is an invariant, a constant for the growth of the entire system of the world's population, and it stems from the self-similarity of the process of growth. Given that growth and development are interwoven, these cycles define the temporal structure of the entire history of humanity, from ancient times to our era.

"The theory of growth and the estimates of demography both lead to the extremely important conclusion that a stabilization of the world's population at the level of 9–11 billion people is approaching. A world in which, with zero growth and stabilization of population numbers, a new epoch in the history of humanity will begin."

The Transformation of Time in History

When describing the history of mankind, the nonlinear growth trend in the world's population leads to a situation in which development itself transforms the flow of its own speed of time. This is primarily seen in an exponential shortening of the duration of historical periods, where the relativity of time in history reveals itself to be essential in terms of understanding growth (Figure 2). The Ancient World lasted about three thousand years, the Middle Ages one thousand, Modern Times three hundred years, and Recent History a little over a hundred years. Historians, primarily I.M. Diakonoff[22], have noted this decrease in historical duration in the extent of the development of humanity [9].

However, to understand the consolidation of time, it should be compared to the dynamics of population growth. In the case of hyperbolic growth, the relative speed of the population's growth is inversely proportional to antiquity—time, counting forward from the critical epoch of the year 2000. Thus, two thousand years ago the population of the world grew by 0.05% per year, 200 years ago by 0.5% a year, and 100 years ago by 1% a year. The most recent cycles, ending with the contemporary singularity of growth and global demographic revolution, were already cited. Humanity reached the maximum speed of relative growth of 2% per year in 1960 – 35 years before the maximum absolute increase in the world's population (Figure 18).

This periodization of exponentially increasing cycles can easily be extended into the past, until the very first singularity connected with the appearance of man, gifted with intelligence, which enables us to calculate the entire sequence of cycles and compare it with data received by generations of historians and anthropologists with the establishment of the periodization of the entire history of humanity over 4.3 million years.

Since a great amount of literature is devoted to periodization and the chronology of humanity's history, the author turned to generally accepted views about changes of cultures and technologies in accordance with data about history and anthropology for the development cycles identified, given in Table 2.

The picture we arrive at is in line with the data put forward by historians to an astonishing degree of accuracy, despite all the difficulties involved in establishing when these periods took place, especially in the Stone Age. A degree of uncertainty arises in the last epoch of the Stone Age—the Mesolithic period. There is almost no reliable data enabling us to establish the population in the epoch of the Stone Age with any accuracy.

---

[22] Igor Mikhailovich Diakonoff was a Russian historian, linguist, and translator and a renowned expert on the Ancient Near East and its languages.

The dating of transitions is therefore determined by technological and cultural markers.

The acceleration of growth leads to a situation whereby after every cycle, the remainder of time for the rest of the developments is practically equal to half of the preceding stage. For example, after the lower Paleolithic period, which lasted a million years, there were half a million years to go before our times, and after the millennium of the Middle Ages, 500 years passed. By this moment the historical process had accelerated by a thousand times.

The transformation of the duration of the historical process can also be seen in the fact that the histories of Ancient Egypt and China lasted millennia and are recorded in terms of dynasties, whilst the tread of Europe's history was determined by individual reigns. The Roman Empire, as it was described by the English historian Edward Gibbon[23], disintegrated over a period of a thousand years—from the fall of Rome in 476 to the fall of Constantinople in 1453 [10]. Contemporary empires rarely take such a long time to disintegrate: the British Empire fell apart in the space of a decade, and the Soviet Union even faster than that. With the unstable auto-model, growth occurs with a compressed form of development, whereby the speed of the historical process increases as the time of demographic transition draws nearer, leading inevitably to a crisis of growth.

Thanks to the deceleration of time in the past, one's own duration of development is constant, whilst the scale of the systematic time of historical development changes. For this specific reason, it should be examined in a logarithmic representation of times, so as to add evenness to the picture of development. Anthropologists, reflecting on the entire range of times in the Stone Age, from a million years of the Lower Paleolithic period to ten thousand years of the Neolithic period, traditionally referred to the logarithmic scale of time; in the context of the theory this follows on from the very dynamics of growth.

---

[23] Edward Gibbon was an English historian and Member of Parliament. His most important work, *The History of the Decline and Fall of the Roman Empire*, was published in six volumes between 1776 and 1788

The Problem of Time in History

To understand the development of the population of Earth as a self-organizing system, we should refer to views about our own internal time and its uninterrupted connection with the process of development and growth. These questions for evolving systems were examined in studies of the irreversibility of development, expressed using the image of an 'arrow of time' by Ilya Prigogine[24] [28].

The fundamental monograph by I.M. Saveleva and A.V. Poletaev[25] *History and Time: in Search of the Lost* [25] is dedicated to the problem of time in history. They put forward two concepts for time—absolute, Time-1, and historical, Time-2 – for a self-organizing system, as which the time taken for the development of the Earth's population should be seen. For the growth of the population of Earth, Time-2 is a logarithm of Time-1.

The appearance of one's own Time-2 in history is analogous to the way in which, in Einstein's general theory of relativity, the evolution of a gravitating system determines the flow of time itself and the local course of the clock. The concept of the internal time of development was aptly defined by Frans Jozeph Radermacher as *Eigenzeit*—one's own time, Time-2.

The concept of absolute Time-1 was best formulated by Newton, when he created the basis of classical mechanics,

> Absolute, true mathematical time in and of itself and of its essence, without any relationship to anything external, flows equally and is otherwise referred to as duration.
>
> *Relative, apparent or ordinary time is a measure of duration, either exact or changing, attainable by means of feelings, external, progressing by means of some form of progression in the extent of duration, used in every-day life instead of true mathematical time, such as: an hour, a day, a month, a year [26].*

---

[24] Viscount Ilya Romanovich Prigogine was a Belgian physical chemist and Nobel Laureate noted for his work on dissipative structures, complex systems, and irreversibility

[25] Andrey Vladimirovich Poletaev was a Russian economist and historian who worked with Saveleva on a series of famous works.

Under the influence of Henry Bergson's[26] ideas about the nature of the relativity of time, French historians and structuralists developed an understanding of duration. It is associated with the process of transformations in the system itself and reflects ideas about historical time, different from what is shown on clocks measuring worldly, Newtonian, time. In this way, the concept of *longue durée* emerged–a space of duration from which, whilst immersed in it, the historical process should be examined. Logarithmic Time-2 is counted from $T_1 = 1995$–highlighted in the entire history of humanity as the moment of demographic revolution (Table 2).

For the surroundings of the time of transition of the Earth's population, it is best to transfer to a linear grid for T and N, when with the passing of demographic transition, the linear connection between time and the population of the world is preserved. The same happened in the distant past, with the appearance of the primary population of humanity, endowed with intellect, when the population under anthropogenesis in the first approximation grew linearly.

The Neolithic Period was the time when, ten thousand years ago, the development of agriculture and concentration of the population in villages and cities replaced the times of wide dispersal of populations. In the logarithmic concept the Neolithic Period is found right in the middle of epoch B. Thus, in the time limits stated, the Neolithic Period belongs to history, and not prehistory—the Stone Age, which corresponds to contemporary views of historians and anthropologists.

It would be instructive to note that the logarithmic transformation of time can be observed in music as well. In musical notation, the fundamental flow is in the course of execution—clock time is linear and its tempo can change in fairly narrow limits from *Lento* to *Presto*. The height of the tone is depicted in logarithmic view and usually covers ten octaves from 20 to 20000 Hz, or fluctuations per second, when the period of fluctuations changes a thousand-fold—from 0.05 seconds to 50 microseconds. These limits take shape by a range of frequencies, perceived by the human ear. For the duration of a note length itself, there

---

[26] Henri-Louis Bergson was a major French philosopher, influential especially in the first half of the 20th century

are no such limits, except the will of the composer and performer, or, ultimately, the tolerance of listeners.

Table 2. The history of humanity in a logarithmic scale of time.

Epoch	Period	Date, years	Number of People	Cultural cycle	ΔT, years	History, Culture, Technology
C	T_1	2150	10×10^9	Stabilization of Earth's population		Transition to the limit 11×10^9 Change of age-specific distri-bution—aging
		2050	9×10^9			Globalization
		2000	6×10^9	Universal demograph-ic transition	45	Urbanization
B	11	1955	3×10^9		45	Computers, Internet Nuclear energy
	10	1840	1×10^9	Newest history	125	World wars Electrification and wireless communication
	9	1500		New history	340	Industrial Revo-lution Book printing
	8	500 BC		Middle Ages	1000	Geographic discoveries Fall of Rome, Muhammad
	7	2000 BC	10^8	Ancient World	2500	Christ, "Axial Age" Greek civiliza-tion, India, China, Buddha and Confucius
	6	9000		Neolithic	7000	Interfluves, Egypt Writing, cities, bronze Domestication

Epoch	Period	Date, years	Number of People	Cultural cycle	ΔT, years	History, Culture, Technology
	5	29000	10^7	Mesolithic	20000	Ceramics, Microlith
	4	80000		Mousterian	51000	Population of America Languages, shamanism
	3	0.22 million	10^6	Acheulean	140000	*Homo sapiens* Speech, cultivation of fire
	2	0.60 mil		Cheulean	380000	Population of Europe and Asia Hand axe
	1	1.6 mil	10^5	Oldowan	1000000	Beachy (oldowan) culture, chopper *Homo habilis*
A	T_0	4–5 mil 7–5 mil	(1)	Anthropogenesis Emergence of HAR1 F gene	2800000	Beginning of socialization Development of hominids with large possibilities of brain and consciousness

Fundamental views about time developed in modern physics find their application with the interpretation of processes in history. This allows for the opportunity to explain the appearance of structures in the temporary global development of humanity. In the processes of development and growth, temporary epochs exceed the borders of countries and continents as a result of the social evolution and self-organization of humanity, subordinate to collective interaction and possessing a general informational nature. Specifically these incidences of metahistory became the fundamental object of a developed theory and present the field on which the dramas of specific events in the lives of peoples unfold.

Breaks and Demographic Transitions

A special role in metahistory is played by the disruptions, changes to the regimes of growth and revolutions with which, as with punctuations, the life line of humanity is marked. The following section is dedicated to a study of the nature of these events.

Transitions, different, according to scale, which can be classified by their strength, take place in an unbalanced evolving system in the regime with intensification, as a result of the explosive growth of humanity. We notice the transitions between cycles at an uninterrupted speed of growth by means of changes in culture. Just as in a basic equation, growth is equated to development, so culture and development proved to be bound up in demographic growth, highlighting the continuity of growth in quantity with the processes of culture.

> *"Transitions, different, according to scale, which are connected with the development of culture, occur in an unbalanced evolutionary system, growing in the regime with intensification, as a result of explosive growth."*

In context, the concept of culture should be interpreted broadly, as everything connected with the mind and consciousness, including technology and economy, education and art, science and religion. This connection is specifically expressed through global informational interaction, defining the synchronized development of the demographic system of humanity.

A global demographic revolution is when a sudden burst of speed of growth takes place from an asymptotic departure from infinity to zero speed and stabilization of the population of the world. This must lead to very significant changes in the development of humanity. Indeed, under this classification, the demographic transition is the strongest in the entire history of humanity. This points to a character and scale of changes, through which we must live in the differing dimensions of our consciousness and existence. Demographic revolution is similar to a strong break in an intensified wave of a supersonic flow of gas or explosion, a phase transition in a condensed environment, approaching critical temperature—an event that is well known in physics.

To be able to illustrate the processes that are taking place during breaks in development, one can see analogous events, which are examined in a completely different field. Many people may have observed that in mountain rivers, during rafting of the forest, when a reserve of water is cast off in riverheads, a steep ledge appears which runs down the river with an abrupt drop in the water level, and then the river itself runs in a calm, undisturbed lower flow.

The break happens because the speed of the current, which depends on the depth of the water, passes over a greater difference in depth than in shallower water. That is why the break outruns the undisturbed flow of the river. In this event, typically nonlinear, it can be seen that the break itself gives rise to the new conditions and provides the possibility of flow of the forest down the flow of the river, which overflowed due to the will of a timber floater.

The development of humanity itself is similar to this. After the demographic revolution it cannot follow its former regulations any longer, and this leads to changes in the historical process. Moreover, the burst of growth under a demographic transition is accompanied by a local breach of the smoothness of the movement. As with the river in the field of the break, so under demographic transition a zone of turbulence arises—a difference in depth with a sudden change of the regime and a breach of the ordered movement.

And so in the epoch which Landry justifiably described as a revolution, this is marked by events of disintegration of order, with a sharp change from one type of movement to a new one. Just as in the phased transition, there is swift **reform** at such times, with the old structures falling and being replaced by a new order. The duration of transitional processes in the field of the break is defined by the internal and local events in the historical processes of changes. It is precisely because of the stormy and unstable dynamics of movement in the field of breakage that the time we live through is so difficult and uncomfortable.

Analogies of demographic transition with bursts and the gradual approach of chaos in the zone of transition should help us to understand the difficulties and the specifics of the time that we are living through, when neither linear models, nor the habitual 'business as usual' scenario are applicable. According to this conclusion, the scale of global changes demands a new and thorough understanding. The political will, as well as the major decisions of the authorities at the unique juncture in global history in which it was our destiny to live, are dependent on this understanding more than anything else.

In the epoch of demographic revolution, the scale of significant social changes occurring in the course of human life became so significant that neither society as a whole nor the individual has time to adjust to the stresses caused by changes to the world order: mankind, as never before, "hurries to live, and hastens to feel."

Given that the transition is of a fundamental nature, connected primarily with going over the limits of the speed of growth of the system, it is also reflected in the phenomena of culture and consciousness, accompanied by a collapse and a crisis of values which were formed over many centuries and became established as the moral norms of society, anchored by faith and by the tradition of social experience.

> *"In the epoch of demographic revolution, society as a whole and the individual person don't have time to adapt to stresses from sudden changes of world order."*

In this case, as in any complex system, naïve reductionism and casual analysis with simple mechanisms for exiting a crisis not only fail to explain the nature of transition, but also prevent the overcoming of it, since direct outer resource measurements turn out to be ineffective. That is why a fundamental understanding of the nature and the scale of all that is happening in the epoch of abrupt changes is so necessary. As was noted, the entire path of the uneven global development of humanity is best seen on a double logarithmic grid, responding to the dynamics of growth, where all the auto-model processes are reflected in straight lines (Figure 9).

Incidentally, the auto-model growth of humanity includes five procedures—from a hundred thousand in the initial population in the Lower Paleolithic, 1.6 million years ago, to the 10 billion that is expected after the demographic revolution. At present, the size of the population of developed countries has already stabilized at the level of one billion,

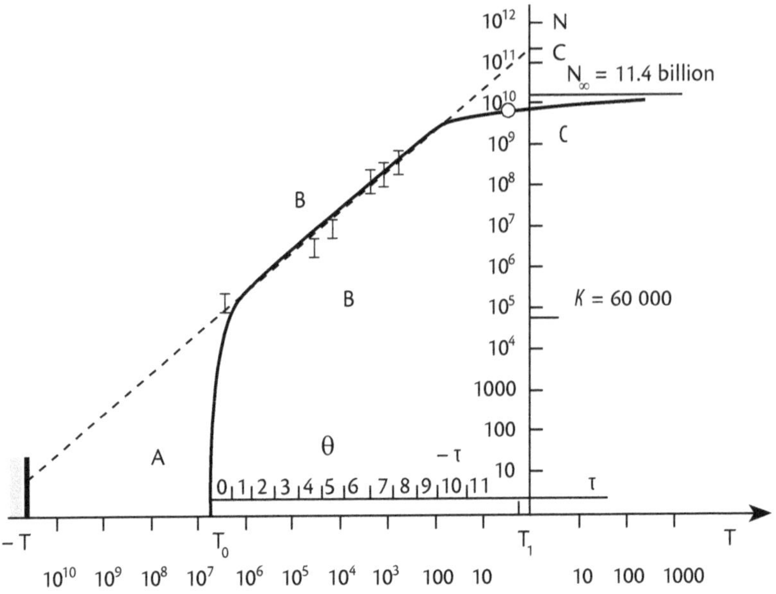

**Figure 9. The growth of the population of the world
from the origin of humans to the foreseeable future**

The graph is built in the double logarithmic scale Lg T – Lg N,
which corresponds to the dynamics of mankind's development.
Demographic cycles derived as $\theta = \ln t$.

and in these countries we can see an order of events which in a short time
will make themselves known in countries which are currently developing.

These processes will envelop all of humanity when the global
demographic transition will end and a new epoch of humanity's history
will begin. In the first approximation, the conversation can focus on
the null growth, calmer speed and new temporary structure, apparently
connected with the scale of generations and the appearance of new
temporary sociocultural structures.

It is therefore important to understand what awaits us and how the
development of humanity will change after the arrival of population
stability on a global level, the approach of which is indicated by the
theory, as well as the foresight of demographers. Moreover, a change to
the paradigm for the growth of humanity itself will begin, as well as the

purpose of its development, not only the 'end of history,' as was figuratively supposed by Francis Fukuyama[27] [12] following Oswald Spengler[28] [47].

"After the transition, history, naturally, will keep going, but there is every reason to suppose that its development will be completely different."

Factors of culture and consciousness, expressed in collective interaction, define the development of humanity as well as the advanced crisis. Furthermore, this global crisis will come to an end in less than a hundred years and, as was already pointed out, in the strength of its swiftness presents many more uneasy threats, related to energy sources, ecology, or climate change.

The exhausting of fuel, be it gas or oil, and change of technology in energetics happens gradually, as can be seen in the spread of nuclear or alternative energy today. Similarly, expected changes to the climate will occur gradually, in contrast to humanity's reaction to the global demographic transition, which has already begun, primarily in the socioeconomic field.

The consequence of globalism of the nonlocal quadratic law of growth began not only with the synchronization and narrowing of the global demographic transition and the irreversibility of growth, but the inevitable lag of isolators as well, which for a long time turned out to be cut off from the rest of the mass of humanity, in general concentrated in Eurasia. Therefore, the prolonged isolation of the population in comparison with the time of remoteness, undoubtedly, when there is a break away from the global community, to delayed development.

---

[27] Yoshihiro Francis Fukuyama is an American political scientist, political economist, and author. He is best known for his book *The End of History and the Last Man* (1992), which argued that the worldwide spread of liberal democracies and free market capitalism of the West and its lifestyle may signal the end point of humanity's sociocultural evolution and become the final form of human government.

[28] Oswald Arnold Gottfried Spengler was a German historian and philosopher of history whose interests included mathematics, science and art. He is best known for his book *The Decline of the West*, published in 1918 and 1922, covering all of world history. He proposed a new theory, according to which the lifespan of civilizations is limited and ultimately they decay

The unchangeable law of growth under examination is applicable only for a whole exclusive system such as the interconnected population of Earth. Therefore, the law of quadratic growth cannot be extended to fit one particular independent country or region. On the contrary, the development of each country should be observed against the backdrop of growth in the population of the entire world.

> *"It is self-evident that any isolated society, cut off from humanity for an extended period of time, will remain on its own path of growth and development."*

The cohesion and evolution of humanity should be understood in general, as a result of customs, beliefs, views, acquired skills and knowledge, passed on from generation to generation with long-term teaching, education, and a person's upbringing as a member of society.

Thus, if in biological, Darwinian evolution, the information is passed on genetically and is consolidated by selection, then in social evolution the mechanism of inheritance is carried out more exactly by Lamarck's process, through epigenetic inheritance—by means of a direct transfer to the next generation of the information acquired, after being broadened through education, culture and science. In this, and the other model of evolution, these processes are played out with development of the population, which in our case of social evolution is the entirety of humanity. This development takes place in the open system and is self-increasing, ending in demographic revolution when *Homo* finally reaches its maximum numbers and can no longer support hyperbolic growth in the regime with intensification.

The straightforward transfer of acquired information and its spread multiplies—the point of the system of education and means of mass information consists specifically in this, regardless of who conceived them. Before the invention of writing, this might have been an elder, as a carrier of the oral tradition, transmitting myths from long ago passed down through the centuries, later—a chronicler, and now—a director of a television station or a professor in a university. This leads to the fact that social development goes much faster than the biological evolution that took place in the closed system of biocoenosis. If, under biological evolution, the result of selection, species adapt to the surrounding environment, then the development of humanity is in no small measure separate from nature.

All of the processes are subordinated to what we noted as *demographic imperative*—they occur inside the system and possess an informational nature. This follows from the processes' inherent asymptotic character of the explosive development of humanity; in the first approach that does not depend on external factors. More than that, in the strength of the scale itself, the quantity of the population of the Earth itself is exerting more and more pressure on ecological systems and, it seems, even on the planet's climate.

> *"All of the processes are subordinate to the demographic imperative. They happen inside the system and possess an informational nature, managing the development and growth of humanity."*

In the process of the history of social evolution, as in Darwinian evolution, natural selection of more successful local structures in comparison with less viable forms of organization in society is observed. This process can be defined by local resources as well. Therefore, for humanity, the understanding of natural selection can be transformed into the concept of *historical selection*. The appearance of such structures, limited in space and time, essentially matches up to what historians traditionally associate with the concept of civilization [20].

To better understand the nature of the quadratic dependency of the growth of humanity, we should turn our attention to two circumstances. In the Stone Age, mankind provided for itself through hunting and gathering. Later both agriculture and industry provided the necessary conditions for life and the growth of society on all levels of development. Without this, the existence of society itself would have been impossible, as would its growth and development.

There have been periods of hunger and pestilence in the history of humanity. The Great Plague of 1348 caused the deaths of no less than a third of the European population, and in some countries, such as Norway, half the population perished. Wars caused loss on a similar scale. However, humanity on the whole showed exceptional global stability in its growth and development, against the backdrop of which these losses were no more than transient, although tragic, episodes in history. This demonstrates the amazing systematic *vitality* of humanity, persistently following a self-similar hyperbolic trajectory of growth right up as far as demographic revolution.

If this had not taken place and the former development had continued, then in 2010 there would have been 10 billion people, not 6.8 billion. In other words, the demographic revolution had cost humanity more than 3 billion people by the present day. This assessment provides a point of view about the scale of events that occur in the world, by comparison with which many of the concerns of contemporary politicians seem totally insignificant.

Specifically, it is worth recalling the changes to the Earth's climate that humanity lived through in the past. In the graphs in Figure 10, the parameters of the atmosphere of Earth from the end of the Lower Paleolithic to our own days are shown. This data was initially obtained as a result of the processing of cores from silt that were hacked in the continental glacier of the Eastern Antarctic at the Vostok station, which my brother Andrei Kapitsa[29] established.

The station is located at a height of 3450 meters above sea level, at an average annual temperature of –50 °C. At this same location the lowest ever temperature on Earth, –89 °C, was recorded. In these conditions, Andrei Kapitsa and an international group of scientists, having analyzed the cores of ice, succeeded in acquiring unique facts about the paleo-climate on our planet [29].

On the graphs four maximums can be clearly seen, which mark the glaciations of Earth within the period of 110,000 years and the maximum which we are living through at the present time. These graphs of the state of the atmosphere of our planet steadily changed within certain limits, upon which humanity in the time of the Stone Age lived through nine ice ages from the time of the appearance of the first human—more than a million years ago.

---

[29] Andrey Petrovich Kapitsa was a Russian geographer and Antarctic explorer, discoverer of Lake Vostok, the largest subglacial lake in Antarctica.

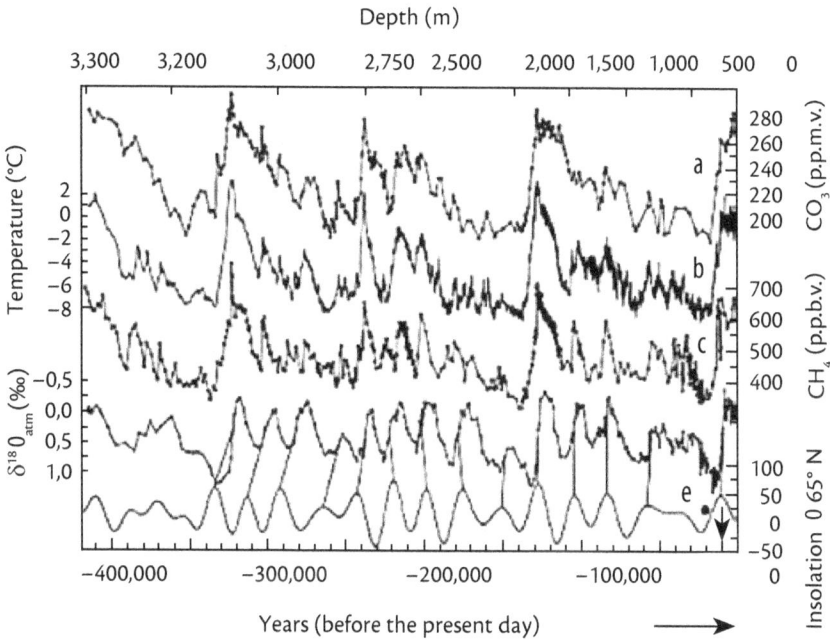

**Figure 10. Climate over the past 420,000 years according
to analysis of cores at the station "Vostok"**

Graphs show: **a** – carbon dioxide content, **b** – temperature, **c** – methane
content, **d** – changes in content of oxygen-18 isotopes, correlating with
temperature, and **e** – insulation for mid-July, calculated for 65 °C North
longitude (V/m²). On the lower linear scale for Time-1 the arrow ↓
points to the beginning of the Neolithic period, 10,000 years ago. On
the logarithmic scale for Time-2 this corresponds to the mid-point of
the entire history of humanity (see Table 2). The time interval stated
only covers a quarter of the total time, from the beginning of the lower
Paleolithic period 1.6 million years ago to our era.

In this epoch glaciers, like pistons, slowly, over the course of 100,000
years, moved at times of cooling in the Northern hemisphere to the
South, and with warming over the course of 10,000 years retreated to
the North. There is every reason to believe that these climate changes led
people in prehistoric time toward continuous migrations, in the course of
which people populated new spaces, when their social consciousness and
technology stood at a much lower level than in our time.

The arrow, which points to the beginning of the Neolithic Period – 10,000 years ago, visually displays how historical time transforms. If in Table 2 the logarithmic view of historical Time-2, the Neolithic Period is located in the middle of the entire continuation of the life of humanity, then on the linear scale of time it turns up on the very edge of the graph (Figure 10).

In these lengthy epochs in the past, the social memory of humanity, the systems of views, customs and habits that define the behavioral instincts of humanity for many dozens of millennia, anchored by hereditary mechanisms of preservation and by transmission of socially significant information were formed and set aside. Thus, as early as in the first stages of the development of humanity, prohibitions appeared—taboos that stand in the way of one or other types of behavior; incest, for example. The ethnic principals of human behavior are therefore deeply rooted and universal. These gradually formed and consolidated their grip to become the first ethnic norms, and later—religious views.

In the present age, the religious map of the world, which historically has often been tied to national culture, forces us to adopt a scientific worldview, based on the views of modern science and which was already a global phenomenon. Without taking into account similar evolutionary processes, it is difficult, if possible at all, to understand the appearance of developed systems and religious views with its intellectual culture and spiritual tradition and the system of scientific views. Before these and other systems of worldviews stands the task of development, a task set by the era of changing landmarks and global demographic transition.

When there is a change of views, primarily religious ones, as a rule, customs from the past live on as relics in the new beliefs and models of perception of the world and of human behavior, as archetypes of something that is often very distant. Folklore, as the universal memory, emerges beyond the borders of time and space, contains the imprints of images from long past eras, which to this day fill the world with epic legends and fairytales—our art and literature. This points to the evolutionary unity of development, which is fixed in man's collective memory in addition to his genetic memory, and which can also reinforce the old stereotypes of behavioral models already at the level of our instinctive responses. These processes are observed by the prominent English biologist and evolutionist,

Richard Dawkins[30] [37]. He, and a host of other scientists, put forward the idea of *memes*[31], which carry cultural information and, just like genes, are passed down from one generation to the next.

Norms of behavior which have been strengthened by being passed down can undoubtedly be changed and transformed when subjected to stress. Destabilization of the genome of this kind is observed in domesticated animals. D.K. Belyaev's[32] observation of foxes, in particular, showed that the stress brought on by captivity led to deep changes not only in their behavior, but even in their coloring, and to seasonal changes in their reproduction cycles.

Therefore, it could be assumed that stress that is caused by demographic transition is capable of influencing the destruction of man's deeply ingrained social instincts. Whereas the consolidation of behavioral instincts in this connection took place over the course of many generations, the disintegration of them, when stress is brought on, occurred very quickly. As the saying goes, '*you don't build anything by breaking things.*'

Only an appeal to the general mechanism of development by means of the transfer of information allows us to reach the breadth of this description on the basis of the model, in which the actual starting point is the total population of Earth. This is the main variable, independent of any particulars whatsoever. Global development is statistically determined and stabilizes near the hyperbolic path of growth with short periods of internal processes, in accordance with the principle of synergy.

The planet's demographic cycles, with reduced duration and synchronized in space, can be observed near this trajectory. The presence of such cycles points to the steadiness of the process of global growth. On the other hand, the entire small-scale historical process in time and in space presents all the elements of dynamic chaos.

---

[30] Clinton Richard Dawkins, FRS, FRSL is an English ethologist, evolutionary biologist and author. He is an emeritus fellow of New College, Oxford, and was the University of Oxford's Professor for Public Understanding of Science from 1995 until 2008.

[31] A meme is "an idea, behavior, or style that spreads from person to person within a culture."

[32] Dmitri Konstantinovich Belyaev was a Russian scientist and academician. He was director of the Institute of Cytology and Genetics of the present day Russian Academy of Sciences from 1959 to 1985.

Thus, as the duration of historical processes decreases on the scale of one's own time of growth, which is equivalent to moving off into the past from the moment of demographic transition, local development becomes more and more chaotic and unstable and therefore unpredictable. This correlation between slow and stable global cycles in mankind's development, by comparison with the fast and chaotic historical processes, is fully analogous to the change of seasons, when there are slow changes and rapid, fickle changes to the weather. Both these phenomena occur in the complex and dynamic systems of the Earth's atmosphere and oceans, just as in the dynamics of growth in its population. It was this difference in the time scales of the history of humanity that Bradel had in mind and emphasized [6].

In the stochastic of history which began and the spontaneity of the market, society should control the external conditions in which the movement of peoples and capital is taking place. On this basis an understanding can be reached as to why the speed of growth is bound to the complexity of the system, with ideas and culture, and not with demographic characteristics—such as the birth rate and death rate, which do no more than describe the process of growth, expressing it through concrete data, and do not give us a full understanding of the reasons for development.

If we turn to the most distant past, then from the basic formula of hyperbolic growth (1) it follows that at the time of the birth of the Universe there must have been 10 people, which is indicated by the trajectory of development, extrapolated to that distant epoch (Figure 9). This can be interpreted either as an 'idiosyncrasy of numbers,' a random event, or as the manifestation of the anthropic principal, according to which life on Earth and the emergence of consciousness itself has a cosmological scale in terms of the time of development. Stephen Hawking, the British physicist and cosmologist, describes this subject:

> We see the Universe such as it is because we exist ourselves. There are two versions of the anthropic principal—weak and strong. The weak version maintains the assertion that in a very large or infinite time and space the conditions necessary for the development of reasonable life can be realized only in some limited fields of space and time. Consequently, conscious beings in these regions must not be surprised that local conditions answer to the demands, necessary for their existence. This resem-

bles a wealthy gentleman, living in rich neighborhood and not seeing the poverty surrounding him.

Thus, we turn to the weak anthropic principal to 'explain' why the Universe has emerged ten billion years ago—specifically this much time is needed for evolution of conscious beings [27].

This question is left open-ended, but the interpretation of the results of modeling in the light of the anthropic principal prompts us to wonder about the fairness of Hawkings' reasoning, and for that reason an extrapolation of the time of development of humanity gives estimates of one order with the same age, if not of the Universe, then of the Solar System.

The results of modeling also show how demographic factors, expressed in the demographic imperative, are now leading to a fundamental radical break in growth. We should also note that during a demographic transition this break leads to sharp crisis in the birth rate and disrupts the economic equilibrium in developed countries [30, 46].

Here a paradoxical situation arises—in the past there were a lot of children, but growth was low (Figure 4). In our time, on the other hand, the growth and reproduction rate of the population in developed countries is limited by a low birth rate. In other words, in an epoch of demographic revolution in the world, the stability of growth is lost, and therefore, in an interconnected system, the transition is followed by a sharp crisis in the development of the world's population.

From this it is also seen that the exhausting of resources is not the cause of the demographic crisis. If this had taken place, then the lack of resources would have led to a gradual and general slowing of growth, which we do not observe. This is not caused either by the crisis in the Western system of values, as suggested by some authors, since this phenomenon is observed in the countries of the East as well, for example in Japan and South Korea.

Therefore, we once again return to the hypothesis that the internal processes of the growth of humanity define its global and century-long development. With this kind of development, social and economic gradients increase all the time, since there is no time to establish an equilibrium. In light of this, the instability of development must be seen as a consequence of the dynamic of growth itself. This growing absence of equilibrium reaches its peak in the epoch of demographic transition with a change to the paradigm of our development, when the processes which contribute to the removal of social tension are unable to keep pace with the rapid changes in society.

> *"The internal processes of humanity's growth as systems determine its global character and century-long development with an ever-increasing imbalance in development."*

Besides economic and social inequality there is also genetic inequality—genetic injustice, which is the focus of special attention from Nobel Prize-winner James Watson[33]. This new factor rose out of the views of modern molecular biological and the fundamental discoveries made by Watson himself. On the other hand, the significance of these sociobiological factors is growing in modern society, with a small number of children born per woman, advancements in medicine and the collapse of the institution of the family itself.

In the next sections, we will turn to the question of how the informational model allows us to examine our development in the foreseeable future. This exposition will inevitably be fragmented; however, its meaning consists in demonstrating that a collective analysis of the growth of humanity opens up new possibilities for researching human nature and the history of mankind.

Birth Rate, Aging, Migration

The modeling of humanity's growth gives us the opportunity to turn to the problems of our time and the processes that are taking place in Russia. Specifically, responsible governance of society and 'engineering of the future,' demand an understanding of the scale of the current revolution, primarily our approach to consciousness and culture, including science. In

---

[33] James Dewey Watson, KBE, ForMemRS, is an American molecular biologist, geneticist, and zoologist, best known as a co-discoverer of the structure of DNA in 1953 with Francis Crick.

light of this, material development and, to an even greater extent, the push for a consumer society cannot be seen as the priority goal of development, as they were in the recent past.

> "The responsible governance of society and 'engineering of the future' demand an understanding of the scale of the current revolutionary epoch."

Whereas in developed countries of the so-called 'golden billion' a sharp fall in growth can already be seen, during which the population is not replaced and ages rapidly, in the developing world the opposite picture is observed at the present time. There, where young people are in the majority, the population is growing rapidly [3] (Figure 11). In developing countries this transition affects more than 5 billion people, a number which will double once the global transition is completed in the second

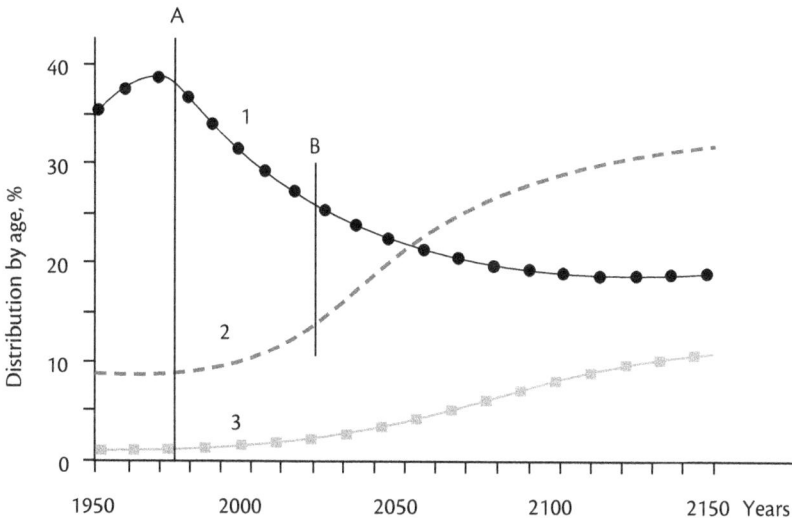

Figure 11. Aging of the world's population of the world during the demographic revolution of 1950–2150 (according to UN data)

1 – age-related group younger than 14, 2 – older than 65 and 3 – older than 80. A – distribution of age-related groups in developing countries, B – and in developed counties in 2000.

half of the 21st century. This process itself is occurring twice as quickly as in Europe and other developed countries.

The development of the economy in China is striking in its intensity: it has grown for the past few decades by more than 10% annually. Production of energy in the countries of Southeast Asia is increasing by 7–8% a year, and the Pacific Ocean is becoming the planet's latest 'Mediterranean', after the Atlantic Ocean and the Mediterranean Sea itself. The premise for the development of systematic instabilities can be seen in this swift growth, for which we received warning in the shape of the financial-economic crisis of 2008.

One of the consequences of the demographic revolution was a sharp fall in the number of children per woman in developed countries. Thus, in Spain and Italy this number stands at 1.20; in Germany—1.41; in Japan—1.37; in Russia—1.3 and in Ukraine—1.09, at a time when, in order to keep up a simple reproduction of the population, an average of 2.15 children for every woman is required—nearly one child more on average than at the present time. Thus all of the wealthiest and most economically developed countries, which 30–50 years earlier lived through a demographic transition, proved to be inadequate at their main function—reproduction of the population; this is the strongest signal that demography can give us [5, 9].

The paradox of the demographic transition lies in the fact that in the past there were many children born per woman; however, growth depended not on the number of children, but only on the small difference between the birth rate and the death rate. This difference, as a measure of growth, determined our systematic development based on the stability of the trajectory of hyperbolic growth from the distant Paleolithic era to the beginning of the 20th century.

"All of the wealthiest and most economically developed countries which in the past lived through demographic transition ended up inadequate in their main function—reproduction of the population."

Thus, as we draw closer to the epoch of demographic transition, the number of children decreases all the time, and when the demographic transition begins, the total number of children falls so far that with the sharp change in growth and development, this has led to the modern crisis of the birth rate—the sharpest contradiction of the 'developed' world, when the 'connection between the times has been broken' (Figure 4).

This is contributed to, as pointed out earlier, by the general crisis in society's mechanisms of organizing itself, as expressed in the collapse of traditional values in the modern world. The objective result of the demographic revolution is a change in the correlation between the elderly and young people, which has led to an extreme stratification of the world along age-related lines.

Specifically, young people who have received an education, but been unable to find work, are often the first to become active in the epoch of demographic revolution, and become a powerful factor in historical development. The stability of the world depends to a large extent on where it concentrates its efforts. Will the younger generation, who often move from the villages to the cities, become the proletariat of the industrial revolution or soldiers fighting in wars and revolutions? Not the working class, but a 'Taliban' of the regions, like in Pakistan and Afghanistan, North Africa and Central Asia, where these contradictions in our 'soft underbelly' are quick to form. There the demographic explosion, the availability of raw energy materials and a crisis in the water supply led to a tense situation in the very center of Eurasia.

By the end of the demographic revolution in the late 21st century, there will be significant aging of the population of the world. If immigrants also have fewer children, and if there is less of what is required for the reproduction of the population, then this situation could lead to a crisis of humanity on a global scale. However, we can suppose that the crisis of the population's reproduction was a reaction to the stress caused by the demographic revolution and for that reason, perhaps, it will be overcome in the foreseeable future once the revolution has ended and humanity goes through a transition to a sustainable, stationary state, because of the stabilization of the world's population (Figure 12).

In this description of the event of transition, we are faced with the above-mentioned difficulty of clarifying the cause/effect relationship in developing complex systems. An example of this paradox is the question: which came first, the chicken or the egg? This dilemma can be solved by

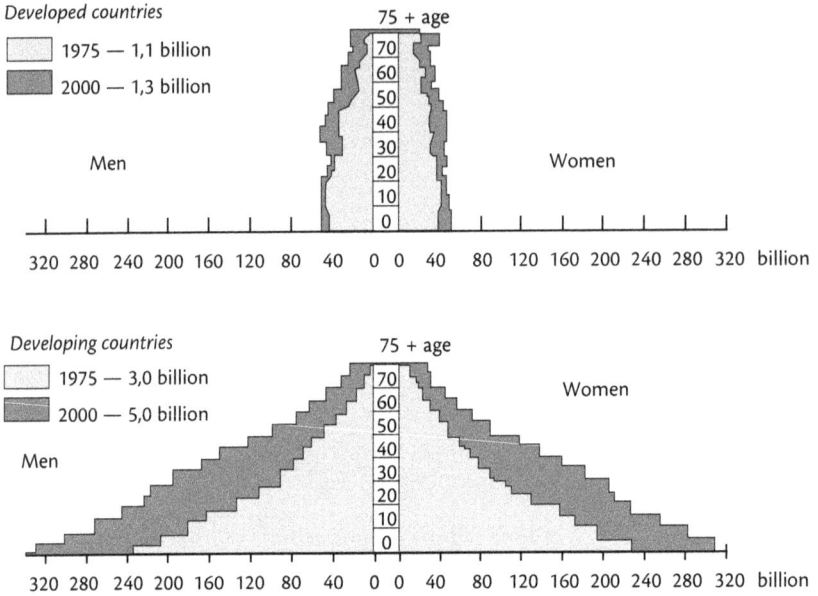

Figure 12. Distribution of the population of the world by age and gender

examining the process in time with evolution and the gradual appearance of ovipositor animals, but it cannot be solved in a statistical system of views.

In the same way, when we attempt to describe the systematic behavior of humanity, the same difficulty appears. It is seen in the issue of which variable—time T or quantity of the population of the world N – is the independent variable. Before the transition of the population, N was dependent on the variable of time, whilst after the transition N becomes a kind of independent variable on which time depends, which overturns the views of cause/effect relationships in the developing global system of the population of the world.

This qualitative difference expresses the nonlinear process of the evolution of complex systems. Hence, when they are being modelled, their development should be seen not as a small nonlinear revolt in a linear system; rather, from the very outset, one should proceed based on the non-linear law of quadratic growth, which cannot be reduced to the sum of the linear processes.

The current era has seen a remarkable increase in the mobility of nations, estates and people. As the countries of the Asia-Pacific region are enveloped by powerful migration processes, so too are other developing countries. The movement of the population occurs inside countries, primarily from the villages to the cities, and between countries, and reflects the destabilization of the demographic system. In the 19th and 20th centuries, at the time of the peak period of growth of Europe's population, immigrants headed towards the colonies and the New World, and in Russia—to Siberia and afterwards to the republics of the Soviet Union. This, without doubt, contributed to their economic growth. However, large movements of people have now emerged, changing the ethnic composition of the mother country; this has become an essential factor in the economy and could lead to the disturbance of the ethnic structure of the country's population, as formed over time. A considerable number of immigrants are illegal and fall outside federal jurisdiction. In Russia there are 10–12 million such people. This causes a complex set of problems, demanding a separate study.

Migration and the movements of those who move to Russia is connected not only to economic factors, but also to the relatively high level of education of some of the immigrants. There are fewer of them than there are guest-workers (*gastarbaiters*), most of whom carry out unskilled labor; but their role is significant from both an economic and social point of view.

> *"The consequences of migration and changes to the traditional ratio of ethnicities may become a source of increasing social tension."*

In these processes, the role of ideas is important: these ideas can hold sway over people's minds and govern their behavior, and in a system of moral norms and values which are formed and consolidated by tradition over a long period of time. In an epoch of rapid change, this time simply does not exist. Therefore, with demographic revolution taking place in a range of countries, including Russia, a break-up of social consciousness and control takes place, the authority and responsibilities of the administration are eroded, and corruption and organized crime grow.

A significant factor, primarily in the moral crisis, has been the loss of trust. This is happening on various levels—from trust between people and within the family, to our trust in financial institutions, laws, justice and the administration of justice, and finally, in the state itself and in the principles of democracy. The loss of trust points to the destruction of the connections within society, on which, to a considerable extent, its stability and development are based.

In the past, the institution of trust was the church; however, in modern society, the images propagated by the mass media, primarily by the television in our country, only promote an erosion of trust. Furthermore, the past has been subjected to revision: in order to satisfy expedient political demands, concepts such as citizenship, patriotism, loyalty to an army oath, and duty have been revised. Thus a destruction of the historical principles of citizens' trust in the country and society is taking place, which is expressed in an individualization of personality and an atomization of society, with the destruction of historical stereotypes.

Only by examining the development of humanity as a whole, in a study with broad time and space limits, did it prove possible to describe the entire process of history in the past and outline the nature of its development in the foreseeable future.

The view of the past set out above is not one that is complete; however, it gives us a conceptual and qualitative basis for forming judgments about the possible paths of our development. The author is convinced that this mutual enrichment of the social and human sciences, and those sciences which are convinced of their objectivity and genuine nature, will help us solve the problems we currently face.

This is why in the foreseeable future we will have a transition to a new paradigm for the development of humanity, a transition to a society in which knowledge and our system of understanding nature and society will define our development. It is for precisely this reason that a change of goals and values in the life of humanity—one that is just as abrupt as the change to the rate of growth—must occur.

"Those who cannot imagine the past cannot count on being able to foresee the future."

To conclude this account of the analysis of the growth of the population of the Earth as a system, we will emphasize the fact that population quantity is a visible change that determines growth and acts as a natural measure of our development. This is expressed in the autonomous equation of growth (2), which allowed us to describe our development quantitatively with broader scope. It is on this basis that we are going to depart from partial models in an interdisciplinary experiment involving the development of a general theory of development of humanity.

What Does the Model for Understanding History Give Us?

Energetics and Economics of Humanity

In the framework of the views that form the basis of the model, the gross consumption of resources can be assessed as the level of humanity's development. The greatest interest is presented by the comparison of growth of the population with the growth of the consumption of energy as the main resource of humanity. The consumption of energy determines all the possibilities for the development of society: the provision of food, the level of industrial production and transportation, the ability to build things and solve environmental problems that have emerged as a result of our activity.

As a criterion of development, energy is remarkable because of the fact that it can be measured and expressed in numerical terms. This means that energy is similar to population numbers as an objective criterion of growth. However, reliable statistical data has only been available since the time of the industrial revolution, from the beginning of the 19th century. A detailed examination of the relationship between the population growth of the world and global consumption of energy in its various forms has been undertaken by John Holdren[34] (Figure 13).

---

[34] In 2009, US President B. Obama appointed professor of Massachusetts Institute of Technology, J. Holden, as the adviser in sciences.

According to economists' estimates, the energy sector accounts for a quarter of the world's global economy. The surpassing, quadratic dependency of the population on the manufacturing of energy looks like it will remain. Between the middle of the 19th century and the end of the 21st century, the population of the world will grow tenfold—from 1.13 billion in 1850 to 11 billion in 2100, and the consumption of energy will increase one hundredfold—from 0.69 to ~60 TWt; however, the speed at which the world's population is growing, due to the demographic transition towards the end of the 21st century, will fall significantly. It is clear that in forecasts such as this, the consumption of energy is connected to population numbers, not the speed of growth, which will fall following the demographic transition.

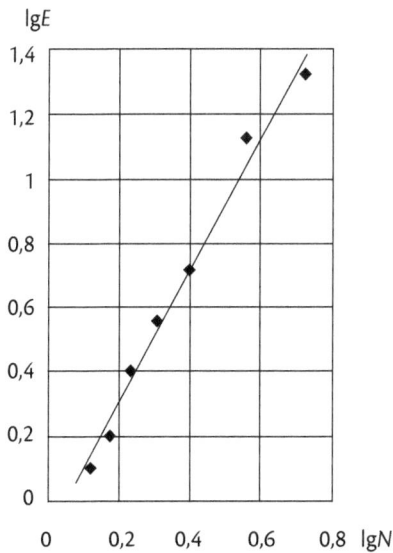

**Figure 13. Global population growth
and energy consumption (1850–2005)**

At present there are indications that the speed of growth of energy production is slowing, and this is especially noticeable in developed countries as a consequence of the dawn of a post-industrial society [31]. Increasing importance is being attached to energy savings. In their monograph at the

Club of Rome, the *Factor of the Four*, Lovins[35] and Weizsacker examine the modern capabilities of energy-saving technologies [42]. The two Swedish scientists suggest that energy consumption can be decreased not by a factor of 4, but by a factor of 10!

However, it is not so much about the energy-saving technologies, as about the realization of such programs through the conversion of industry and in the change of attitude towards the value of energy. Thus, at the European Parliament's instigation, measures are being implemented to limit the use of incandescent bulbs, which are 5–10 times less effective than fluorescent lamps or modern LED lights.

In other words, in this most important problem, the realization of technical solutions is to a considerable extent predetermined by the social side of the matter. This is why it is fitting to remember the historical example of one of Lenin's slogans, "Communism is Soviet power coupled with the electrification of the entire country," which was formulated in different historical circumstances, when for the first time the correlation between politics and energy had become clear. In the modern era it is important to have political will in the conversion of energy and the modernization of the economy while taking into account the strategic character of such decisions and the long-term investments connected with them.

By the end of the 21st century, the power of the global energy system will have grown by 4.4 times compared to 1990 and will consume 57 TWt. If we take into account the fact that by this time, the rate of growth of the population will have fallen considerably and will be 3 times less than it is now, then the estimate examined should be taken at its highest limit.

The discussion of the issue of whether or not our planet will be able to handle such a burden has turned into a debate in which it is becoming tougher and tougher to distinguish the facts from the trends which come into the equation and which often cause interested customers to perk up their ears. When building a type such as this, ecological demands are of foremost importance. This is expressed in the declaration of the

---

[35] Amory Bloch Lovins is an American physicist, environmental scientist, writer, and chairman Scientist of the Rocky Mountain Institute. He has worked in the field of energy policy and related areas for four decades.

principal of the ecological imperative. The question of the maximum carrying capabilities of our planet is one that has been examined by many authors. An instructive discussion of such views is contained in the collection of the IIASA, *The Future Population of Earth: What can be Proposed Today?* [22]. Cohen's review *How Many People Can the Earth Feed?* is dedicated to estimates of the maximum carrying possibilities of Earth, and it declares that, according to various authors, the maximum population is estimated at between 1 billion (Pearson, 1945) and 1000 billion (Marchetti, 1978) [23].

Heilig showed that the majority of such calculations are made using invalid methods. He suggests that the way the question is posed with regard to the limit of the population is in substantial measure robbed of meaning if it is viewed separately from the evolution of social and economic conditions and the development of science and technology. He comes to the conclusion that based on reasonable estimates, the Earth can support as many as 15–25 billion people for a sustained period of time. After a detailed analysis of the capabilities and limits of agricultural production, Heilig draws the following conclusion:

> If we pay attention to the artistic potential of humans, then there are no foreseeable limits to fundamental natural resources for the production of food, which serve space, water, climate conditions, and solar energy in the investment of the human himself. All of these resources are either unlimited, or may be broadened and used in a more practical way, or altered considerably. Because of this, many experts came to the conclusion that there are no limits to the growth of population.
>
> Therefore, the idea of the "physical limits of growth" is a false concept. It enables technocrats from agriculture to deny fundamental issues facing global food production. This is why more serious arguments than this are needed in order to convince people that global production of foodstuffs has limits and may be restricted [22].

These conclusions are confirmed by the latest statements from the UN's Food and Agriculture Organization (FAO). In connection with estimates of the impact of the role of resources and surrounding environment, the conclusions of prominent modern historian Paul Kennedy are of interest:

From the point of view of environmental activists, the Earth is currently under dual human pressure—an excess of needs and the extravagance of rich developed countries and billions of new mouths, inceptive in a developed world, which, naturally, expect to increase the level of consumption. This led to protectors of the environment such as the World Watch Institute, Greenpeace and the UN Population Fund declaring that it is only a question of time. From their point of view, unless something is done to stabilize the world's population, to decrease the unaccountable consumption of energy, food and other resources, and unless we begin to limit the damage to the surrounding environment as soon as possible, then before long the Earth will be so overpopulated and ruined that we will pay a high price for our neglect.

The point of view which disputes the statement that growth is desirable and that economic development is the best measure of a country's material success calls for sharp objections from economists. Optimists suppose that natural resources are not limited in number and cannot be exhausted. The opposite is more likely—that many resources are created by labor and ingenuity and that in techniques and technologies is the endless reserves of renewal of resources.

The disappearance of some sort of commodity, such as oil, leads to the search for and introduction of new supplies, allowing for the creation of alternative sources of energy. Anxiety over the fall of volume of production of provisions has resulted in discoveries in the field of biotechnologies and the production of agricultural labor has essentially increased. As inaccurate as Malthus was in his predictions, then today's spokesman will also prove to be incorrect concerning our destruction.

Only time will tell which of these two positions will turn out to be more accurate. However, the population of the world was less than a billion when Malthus wrote the first version of his sketch. Now the population of the world will soon reach 7 or 8 billion and could very well surpass 10 billion. If the optimists are correct, then there will simply be more prosperous people living on Earth, even if the distribution of goods is uneven. If the optimists are mistaken, then the human race will suffer from unrestrained economic growth, as a result of which it will lose out as a result of this change to its true habits [36].

In conclusion, we will point out that today, in developed countries, 2–4% of the population could feed the entire country (Figure 14). Furthermore, as experts form the FAO affirm, there are enough space and resources in real time to supply 20–25 billion people with nourishment, and the modern production of consumer products already exceeds demand throughout the world. The problem of consumption consists not in the limited nature of resources, but in the inability to distribute resources on the scale of global humanity. In other words, we are dealing with a socio-economic problem and not with limited resources.

An analogous conclusion can be made with regard to water consumption. The majority of modern sources of energy are composed of so-called non-renewable sources: coal, oil and gas, and, to a certain extent, uranium. These sources of energy are in theory exhaustible, in contrast to water, which circulates in a hydrological cycle and will essentially never disappear. Furthermore, 1/20 of those expenses, which provide the energetic sector of the economy go toward our water supply.

The very accessibility of water means that it can be used in extravagant ways. Thus, in Moscow, there are 3 cubic meters of water available per day for each person living in the city. And for the developing countries, the West's greatest money-saving invention, according to economists, is the flushable toilet—a highly ineffective arched system of irrigation in comparison with polyethylene tubes used to irrigate gardens and vineyards.

With resourceful assessments of limits of growth it is necessary to account for technological progress. One of the areas of criticism of *Limits of Growth* by Medous was given mistaken examples of the exhaustion of resources. Calculations were cited that in 12 years global supplies of silver will be exhausted, the primary consumer of which is cinematography. However, the invention of magnetic and digital recordings fundamentally changed all the technology in this field. On the other hand, the authors of the predictions made the point that with regard to the exhaustion of our aluminum, based upon our explored supplies of bauxite, 7% of the earth's core consists of aluminum and hence its supply is practically inexhaustible.

In the proposed model for growth, there are no such contradictions, since at its foundation lies the informational mechanism of global development, which, throughout the entire course of the history of humanity, proposed socially essential solutions for the scientific and technological problems we face. Furthermore, the history of technical progress has repeatedly shown that many inventions and technologies waited for their time and appeared, like a rabbit out of a magician's hat, when they were needed. This is why the proposed model of growth presents principal bases for an optimistic view of the technological future of humanity, if it copes with socio-economic challenges conditioned by development itself. The transition to the new paradigm of development by a null quantity of growth and criteria of the quality of humanity and the level of the manner of life become the goals of development.

Demographic Revolution and the Crisis of Ideology

An unbalanced societal state is developing as a result of world demographic revolution and the social and economic inequality that comes with it, as is seen in both developing and developed countries. This socio-political crisis is universal in nature and its limited reality, undoubtedly, is the nuclear missile weapon with which several countries are armed. However, all the feebleness of the concept 'I've got power on my side—no need for a brain' were brought to light with the collapse of Soviet Union and the invasion of Iraq, when, despite enormous arms, practically limitless in capacity, ideology in particular—software-based security of politics—turned out to be 'the weakest link' and could not provide a solution to the contradictions that had arisen.

In conclusion, in the modern nuclear world, the assertion made by Clausewitz[36] that "war is a continuation of politics by other means," no longer has its place. The agreement by the organization of strategic weapons is the consequence of the refutation of this assertion by Clausewitz, and practice often supports this for 'minor wars' as well.

---

[36] Carl Philipp Gottfried von Clausewitz was a German-Prussian soldier and military theorist who stressed the "moral" and political aspects of war

In his book, *Limits of Power: The End of American Exceptionalism*, A. Bachevich points to the deep crisis that befell America, the economy of which is in a state of great disarray, and the fact that it has become impossible to support it by exporting capitalism,

> The government, reformed by the president's imperial style, remains democratic in name only. Involvement in endless wars, subordinate to the enthusiasm for military power, became a catastrophe for the political system. These growing problems threaten all of us –Republicans and Democrats. If the country wants to solve these obstacles, then this demands a return to a genuine American approach—the forgotten tradition of realism [39].

President Barack Obama also confirmed the American Exceptionalism that became the symbol for his speeches: "America can do anything it wants."

Indeed, demographic revolution is expressed not only in demographic processes, but also in the fundamental strategic problems and technological aspects of a country's safety and also in many measurements of our existence. On the other hand, this finds its reflection in tendencies of modern art and postmodernism in philosophy, in the inability to provide well-structured answers to the challenges of time.

Drawn from the past, the abstract, and in many ways old-fashioned, concepts of some philosophers, theologists and ideologists retain the meaning, if not the words, of political slogans. There appears an irrepressible desire to 'fix' history and apply the experiences of past centuries to our time.

In science, we see an expansion of pseudo-scientific views—from creationism, astrology and telepathy to mystical teachings and magic. Thus a collapse of the organized structure of thought in modern science is taking place, based not just on tradition and authorities, but more on independent examination and comprehensive testing of the results of observations and experiments. Thus the demographic revolution is accompanied by a demolition of the connection of times, the collapse of organization and the establishment of elements of chaos in sharp crisis of administering to society and the inability to answer the summons of technical progress.

Such problems undoubtedly create anxiety about the ecological condition of our planet.

Such a variety of events, in terms of scale, points primarily to general reasons that appeared in the epoch of global demographic transition, when a growing disparity emerged between *'productive powers and productive relationships.'* On the one hand, this is followed by a growing imbalance in society of the distribution of labor, information and resources, in the local and regional levels as well as on a global scale. Following liberal ideology, and in accordance with the thermodynamic analogy, market relationships could have smoothed out this imbalance.

However, there is not enough time for the alleviation of the imbalances which originated, and the growing meaning of development, based on collective and quadratic informative progress, will hinder such equalizing processes. This does not help the prevalence of local self-organization on the federal organization, either.

Indeed, the development of society, by means of quadratic growth, is a process that is inherently unbalanced and irreversible. This is why, when examining hyperbolic growth, our attention should be focused on the fact that such development is radically different from Walrasian models of economic growth, in which the archetype is the thermodynamic of balanced systems, in which slow and adiabatic processes of development occur. During this, the developing system is situated in a quasi-statistical state, since changes to the characteristic time of growth are small. In this case, the mechanism of the market contributes to the establishment of detailed economic balance, and the processes of exchange, in principal, are reversible, and the notion of property answers to the laws of preservation.

However, these views, in the best case, act locally and do not apply to the interpretation of the irreversible and imbalanced global process of development, occurring with the expansion and multiplication of information. It wasn't in vain that economists, from the times of Max Weber[37] and Joseph Schumpeter[38], marked the influence of non-material

---

[37] Maximilian Karl Emil "Max" Weber was a German sociologist, philosopher, and political economist whose ideas influenced social theory, social research, and the discipline of sociology itself

[38] Joseph Alois Schumpeter was an Austrian-American economist and political scientist

factors in our development, in regard to which Francis Fukuyama recently said:

> *Incomprehension of the fact that the bases of economic behavior lie in the realm of consciousness and culture, leads to a widespread error, according to which material reasons attach to events in society, belonging to their own nature mainly in the area of mind.*

Thereby, the utmost pressure of historical time leads to the time of virtual history, joined with the time of real politics. Time, when the historical process of the manufacture of ideologies and the achievement of economic balance and social justice, earlier took up centuries and many generations, is now intensified and demands a new understanding and not blind service to the paradigm of the flowing politic.

In this consists the fundamental change in the global economic system, and it appeared in the first place as a result of the colossal increase of labor in modern society. So, to produce one mid-class automobile it takes ten hours of labor, whilst a tanker that transports hundreds of thousands of tons of oil is serviced by a team of 30 seamen.

As a result, in developed countries manpower is shifted in the sphere of service. Thus, in 2006 in the USA 1–2% of manpower was employed in agriculture and 17% in industry. In Germany, in 1999, turnover in the field of information technologies became larger than in the automotive industry—a pillar of the German economy (Figure 14).

At the same time, costs excessively grow not only on commerce, but also on service of various mediators, dealers and advertising agents and on other services not connected with this type of work. It is notable that in modern conditions, the speed of the replacement of technologies and the organization of the economy is so great that the education of workers and the replacement of equipment present new demands on the economic system, based on innovation and development on the global scale.

Figure 14 is of considerable interest because it can be seen that few workers provide modern agriculture in the USA, where half of the production is exported and the stability of production is guaranteed by subsidies. In the field of agriculture, science is all the more necessary, primarily applied science and bioengineering, which could be called nanobiology, which operates on the level of the genome. This is in contrast

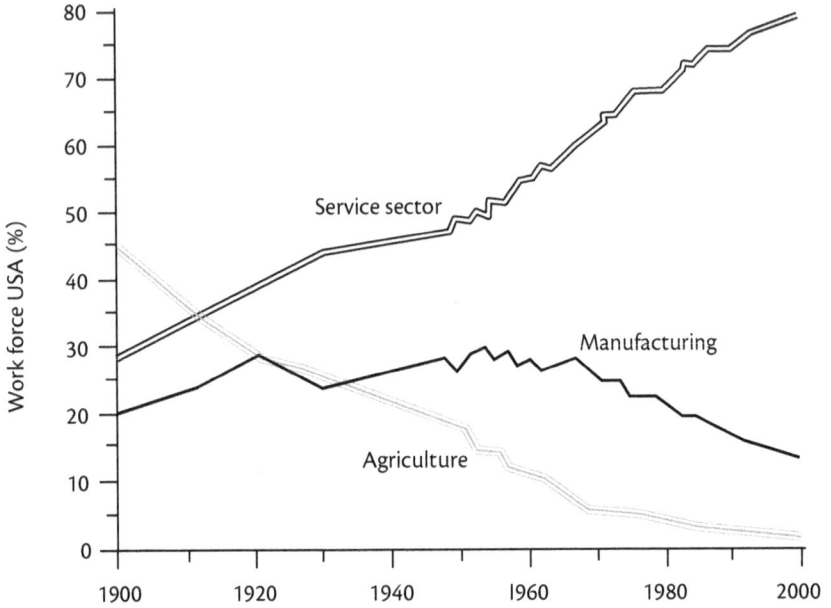

Figure 14. Deindustrialization. Distribution of manpower in the USA in the 20th century by sector of the economy

to microbiology, which is related to microorganisms. It is specifically from nanobiology that we should expect great achievements in medicine as well as in agriculture, or rather in the production of products of nourishment, and we could even bypass our fields and pastures.

The highest growth in the number of scientific workers is seen in China, where the development of sciences became a national priority, and there are currently 150,000 Chinese studying in the USA. Chinese scientists educated in the USA, Europe and Russia are in demand in their homeland, and it is from them that we can expect new breakthroughs in the field of science. The experiences of Japan and South Korea show how quickly countries in the East can modernize. For example, in India export of software products in 2007 reached 50 billion dollars and became comparable with the amounts spent on the purchase of oil—so in economics, intellectual products are the most valuable of all.

We can point out with satisfaction that in 2011 Russia is at last exporting software, primarily search engines such as *Yandex*, realizing that in the global market, advanced technologies are universally recognized achievements of Russian mathematics.

Unprecedented standards of product quality are being seen in this sector of the economy. At the same time, it appears that views related to market stability and intellectual property contradict the fundamental quality of information.

Indeed, when we examine information, it does not stay unchangeable, but multiplies intensely and irreversibly, above all, in systems of science and education. This is why, primarily, in limits of linear models, we approach the impossibility of information of nonlinear quadratic growth to the sum of linear processes, examined in classical mathematical models – Walras's models—of the economy. In such a case, it is necessary to coordinate the long-term model of the development of humanity as a whole with the spatial and temporal limits of a stable economy as problems of econo-physics.

Science, Innovation and Society

In the diagram in Figure 15, the difficulties of the management of science on purely marketing principals can be seen, so far as the time of conversion of the means of production and capital defer by order. Thus, a contradiction between the time of development of the system of knowledge and its support and expansion in society and timely scales of mechanisms and goals of a market-oriented economy appear in the modern world. This is clearly seen in the comparison of the time of realization of the results of fundamental research, motivated by a knowledge of nature, society and humans, and the time of realization of innovation and the development of the economy itself.

With the appearance of fundamentally scientific knowledge, science develops independently as one global event in world culture with general problematic, informational, instrumental and now regular space. Whereas at the beginning of the Modern Age, in the epoch of the Renaissance, at

EDUCATION	→ → → →		**INNOVATION**

| Fundamental Science | → | Applied Science | → | Manufacturing and economy |

TIME:	100 years	10 years	1 year
MONEY ($):	1	10	100
MOTIVES:	knowledge	benefit	development and income

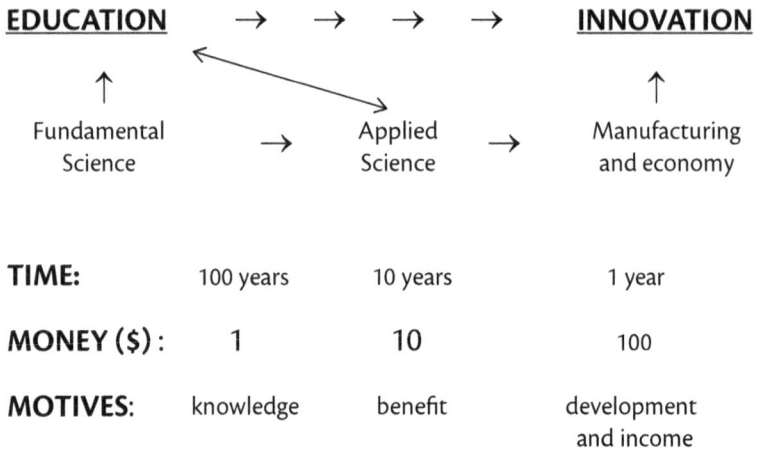

Figure 15. Interaction of science, education and industry in the modern world. The arrows indicate the flow of information

the time of Vesalius[39] and Hugo Grotius[40], Copernicus[41] and Newton, the language of science was Latin, later French and German, it has now switched to English.

The global mechanism of the development of science and the project of the 18th century Enlightenment opened new possibilities for the creation of single wholeness of the picture of the world. Therefore, in the post-industrial epoch, there was such intense demand for a modern interdisciplinary synthesis of our views of the world. Unfortunately, the crisis in the sciences which concern society—all greater specialization, the inheritance of ideologies and the lack of integrating and synthetic

---

[39] Andreas Vesalius was a Barbantian anatomist, physician, and author of one of the most influential books on human anatomy, *De humani corporis fabrica*

[40] Hugo Grotius, also known as Huig de Groot, Hugo Grocio or Hugo de Groot, was a jurist in the Dutch Republic.

[41] Nicolaus Copernicus was a Renaissance mathematician and astronomer who formulated a heliocentric model of the universe which placed the Sun, rather than Earth, at the center

concepts—stands in the way of the development of modern views about the nature of man, especially in his societal consciousness and moral norms.

On the other hand, a considerable cultural and moral experience of humanity is generalized in inheritance and formulated in the ethical norms of global religions. Furthermore, comparative research into norms of morality shows their fundamental unity as regards recommendations on "how to live the right way." Nevertheless, the dialogue of the various faiths between one another and with science is impeded by the differences between them, which are so difficult to overcome, and which are fixed in the absolutism of the static dogmatics of faith.

In the present, attention is fixed on globalization, which implies first and foremost world financial and commercial connections. However, the model of the development of humanity from the very beginning originated in the global nature of the processes of growth. From the time of the paleolith, humans settled all over the planet, but then, slowly but surely, in the course of hundreds of thousands of years, formulated connections, embracing the world. Now this occurs on a different scale of time, faster than in one generation, as was the case with cellular telephones and the expansion of the Internet.

Therefore, the globalization of science and technologies led to the task of national scientific politics becoming a deposit into global science, responding to general high demands. At the same time, the use of the results of global science is impossible without understanding its status and the global processes of development, and this takes shape by measuring the integration of national science into a global unity.

Fundamental science and art culture, for which prolonged priorities are defined by social order and not only by the market with its criteria of fast effectiveness, must be supported by government and managed by society. This leads to the difficulties of the realization of market laws in the field of education, science and innovation under management on the bases of short-term monetarist mechanisms and these contradictions in modern world only intensify. Mostly effective fundamental science influences development through education, hence why the integration of science into the system of education is so important. It is necessary for the development of higher education in Russia in response to the call for innovative development of the country.

Therefore, for example, openings in the field of fundamental knowledge traditionally are not protected by patents. In the practice of world science, fundamental openings are published and immediately become accessible to everyone. Thereby, they show the long-term influence on our worldview. In the end, the same happens with significant events in the art world as well. A highly instructive example is the refusal of the extension of patent rights to the human genome, when, practically at the same time, two groups of scientists decode the genome. One group collaborated under the aegis of UNESCO in a large international project, in which Soviet scientists also participated. The other was organized by an American scientist and entrepreneur, Craig Venter[42], who later strived to "privatize" the results obtained, since this information was of considerable interest to pharmaceutical corporations. However, an international court decided that information about the human genome could not be patented and that all researchers and doctors should be able to access it for free. Arguments about the limits of ownership rights on socially significant objects of culture led to legal regulation, foreseeing that the owner becomes the keeper of these objects by suitable limiting of his rights as the owner.

Experience shows that monopolistic limiting of rights on program security, as seen in the dispute between Windows and Linux, became an obstacle to development, similar to the attempt to spread copyright to such treasures of knowledge as the British Encyclopedia, from which, as it is known, people turned away with time. In the USA, the Massachusetts Institute of Technology provided open access to all publications of their labor and methodical materials. Symptomatically, the French government decided to make admission to all the country's main museums free for the young, thinking that commercialization of high culture is impossible.

The result of limits becomes the growth of pirating and violation of so-called copy rights, or it leads to a break of development, to economic, primarily educational, instability and growing informational monopolism. Such novel social sources of instability can cause new conflicts as well. In these events, the time scale of processes of growth becomes the deciding factor in the assessment of their magnitude and management.

---

[42] John Craig Venter is an American biologist and entrepreneur. He is known for being one of the first to sequence the human genome and for creating the first cell with a synthetic genome

The demographic factor, firmly connected with culture and, in the same way, with ideology, creates special stress in the process of demographic transition, which becomes a constant source of danger as the origin of wars and armed conflicts, particularly in developing countries. Furthermore, the very fact that terrorism occurs is itself an expression of the state of social tension in which we live, as this took place at the peak of demographic transition in Europe in the second half of the 19th century and the beginning of the 20th century. Therefore the "war on terror", with all its cost, is not hitting its target, since terror is the symptom and not the cause of the ills in society. If, instead of the billions which are spent on armed forces, millions could have been set aside for education and public health, then there would not have been any place for terrorism. The pre-war history of Afghanistan and the contiguous republics of the Soviet Union illustrate these conclusions comprehensively.

The goal of the terrorists, first and foremost, consists of drawing attention to their ideals, even at the cost of their own lives. Therefore the exaggerated significance of these acts, making them elements of a psychological battle, if not a war, underlines the role of the informational component in modern politics.

Unfortunately, the attention to such events and positions brought upon by the mass media does not always answer to the interests of society and only leads to the degradation of values in the modern world, since the place that is taken away from these events does not correspond to their significance in the life of a society. George Soros[43] examines these questions in his recent book *The Epoch of Mistakes. The World on the Threshold of Global Crisis* [38]. On the other hand, regular armies more often than not come running into military conflicts, toward terror and secret operations.

It should be emphasized that far fewer people die as a result of terrorism than as a result of road traffic incidents. Thirty thousand people are killed on the roads annually. In Russia, 85 people die each day, which roughly corresponds with the number of passengers in a standard airplane. Global losses from traffic accidents are about one and a half million people a year, or 4,000 people daily, and yet we somehow prefer not to draw

---

[43] George Soros is a Hungarian-American business magnate, investor, and philanthropist. He is the chairman of Soros Fund Management.

attention to these numbers. After all, the people do not suspect every driver on the road of being a potential terrorist!

The role of ideology and the spread of ideas grows by means of active propaganda, commercials and our culture itself. In defense politics, the demographic resources limit the quantity of armies, which demands modernization of the armed forces. With this grows the importance of the technological equipment of the army, as well as the performance of its policing functions, and increases interest in what is generally referred to as the psychological war and the management of consciousness. It is specifically as a result of this that the role of ideology, and the spreading of ideas by means of active propaganda, commercials and the culture itself increases, amongst other things by reference to the views and traditions of religious teaching.

Thus, culture becomes an effective factor in modern politics and information—the tool it uses. In developed countries that have completed their demographic transition, this tendency is already seen in the change of priorities in politics and the way means of mass information are used in modern conflicts.

Of equal importance is the information sector of economics and mass media in education and public health, for the achievement of physical health and spiritual stability in society, which is disturbed during the stressful period of the demographic revolution. Psychological disorders testify to this fact.

The consequences of the processes of humanity's modern history, summoned to show a new understanding of some phenomenon in the past and those which happen at a time of demographic revolution, are listed in this section. The examples and episodes stated, naturally, do not aspire towards any satisfactory, comprehensive analysis and reflection of the scale of the problems. However, they must induce the researchers toward an expansion of our views, taking into account the deep influence of the demographic revolution on our life, considering that the world is undergoing impetuous changes.

Here it may be most essential to tie the global model of our development with the views which dominate the modern economy and sociology, and realize the whole increasing meaning of generalized informational factors, as in modern life and in the history of humanity. On the other hand, the above-mentioned picture of the self-similar and explosive development of humanity shows its connection with the spontaneous appearance of one or two genomes, which define the complexity of our brain.

From these times, as was already pointed out, biologically, the human genus changed little, but it is specifically this that leads to the thought of the possibility of similar root change of the potential of our consciousness. This can happen as a consequence of accidental mutations or as the result of the development of modern methods of influence on the genome. The possibilities of nanobiology and gene engineering are multiplying before our eyes.

The author is turning his attention to these facts; however, he refrains from some prognoses, particularly the one that suggests we should, first and foremost, experience a turn in the development of humanity, after which we can expect some breathing space before a new shock.

Socio-economic Consequences of Growth

The discussion conducted shows that humanity, from the moment of the beginning of hyperbolic growth, developed as a society of knowledge. The fact is that, in essence, economic development is a production of products of nourishment and energy, transportation and connection; habitation and medicine only provided conditions of existence, even if only on the most primitive level, but sufficient for stable development and life support.

Development that is connected with the realization and especially with public realization, although it occurred slowly in the beginning, and then everything sped up in accordance with the law of quadratic growth.

Furthermore, this development itself consisted of pre-determined conditions, such as the speed of growth and the economy, as well as the demand for securing life. However, in the modern age, we are dealing not only with the explosive development of the self-organizing society, but also with the exhaustion of the possibilities for its collective growth, which dominated in the past.

This is a paradoxical conclusion; however, it leads to the deduction, having all the growing importance for understanding the processes, accompanying the critical epoch of that future, which awaits us. With the stabilization of the world's population, further development cannot be connected with quantitative growth, hence it should be analyzed by which way it will go, and in this case, the example of Europe is especially instructive.

That Spengler's[44] eschatological foresight has not been justified yet instills hopes for development, connected with knowledge of culture and science. Development can end and then, begins a period of decline, and ideals of the 'Sunset of Europe' will receive their incarnation. But something else is possible—the qualitative development, the meaning and target of which will become the quality of human and quality of life, and in their basis lies human capital. A series of authors point to this [30].

Many of the countries of Europe, having lived through world wars in the 20th century, and which were the first to pass through demographic transition, are now boldly showing the way in terms of the reorganization of their economic, scientific, technological and political space. Such processes are still to come for other countries. This critical bifurcation, the choice of the path of development, from all its intensity stands before Russia as well.

Nowadays all of humanity is experiencing the exceptional growth of information technologies. As was pointed out, the universal expansion of cellular connections led to the fact that half of the inhabitants of Earth already possess cell phones. The Internet, which now has over a billion users, became an effective mechanism for collective informational network interaction, even the materialization of collective memory, if not the mind of humanity itself, embodied in the technological level of systems of information research, such as *Google* and *Yandex*.

However, access to information is only a first step in the construction of a community of knowledge. Indeed, knowledge by itself is not enough—the target consists of the attainment of understanding. This presents new demands for education, when it is not knowledge, but the comprehension

---

[44] Oswald Arnold Gottfried Spengler was a German historian and philosopher of history whose interests included mathematics, science, and art.

of knowledge, that becomes the main task when educating the brain and mind. It was not for nothing that Vaclav Havel[45] observed, "The more I know, the less I understand."

Simple application of knowledge does not demand deep understanding, and this led to a pragmatic simplification and lowering of demands in the process of mass education.

The problem of instilling an understanding and the artistic beginning connected with this, already as the development of higher steps of intellectual capabilities with greater intensity, will stand before the system of education as well as before society. Everything is connected with upbringing of so-called leading frames.

Thus, after the Great French Revolution, a Polytechnic school was founded in Paris, the graduates of which effectively and corporately ruled the country. After World War II, there was a successful experience in setting up scientific establishments, such as the Moscow Applied Physics Institute and Moscow State Institute of International Relations in the Soviet Union.

The scientists, engineers and diplomats who were educated at these institutions determined the preparation of frames and success of the country in the high technologies of the defense industry and in Soviet of external politics. Furthermore, the specialists educated at these scientific establishments turned out to be important during the time of the creation of the new economy in the 1990s. However, the upbringing of the next generation takes place in the present social order, now already with the account of new tasks, which must become the foundation of innovation of development of the society of the future.

It should be emphasized that the organization of such an institutional establishment does not demand large expense in comparison with the current expenditures and development of higher education. However, their creation demands political will and above all—securing of a high level of preparation and administration of the system of education itself. Unfortunately, in Russia, the necessary steps for the selection and upbringing of administrative frames have not been taken and proper

---

[45] Vaclav Havel was a Czech playwright, essayist, poet, dissident and politician. Havel was the ninth and last president of Czechoslovakia and the first president of the Czech Republic

attention is still not devoted to these problems. At the same time our future as well as the future of humanity depends on them in full measure, to put it in wider context.

Therefore, it is necessary to rise to the next level of differentiation in terms of education and goals and target the best minds and talents, without violation of the principal of the availability of education. It wasn't in vain that the French government recently established the School of Social Sciences for the preparation of administrative frames of republic at the Polytechnic school. By tradition of the Polytechnic school, acceptance into these educational institutions is based on competitive exams, and students are provided with a generous stipend.

Currently, the duration of education is increasing all the time, and often a person's most creative years are the years that correspond more closely to setting up a career and family, are spent on education. Moreover, because of this discrepancy of long education, fast changing in accordance with the demands of society, the next 'lost generation' is emerging, burdened by knowledge but not understanding what they are to do and who needs them.

The difference between information and knowledge is well seen in the difference between the patent that protects the rights for information, and the know-how—the knowledge, implicating the ability to use this information. It is on this understanding, primarily, that the licensed right is based. Hence why it is important to distinguish between the understanding of informational society, and the more capacious understanding of the society of knowledge, as different social categories, and set education and organization of science aspiration toward the society of understanding as the ultimate goal.

The difference between knowledge and understanding becomes apparent in the fact that the country which borrows knowledge by purchasing licenses or technical exploration and even on their successful realization, counting on further leading development, is impossible without their own base in the form of fundamental science. This is necessary for the upbringing of the next generation of scientists, engineers and sociologists, in order to understand the direction of the development of science, born in global science, and for their fast realization.

In modern society, the means of mass media become increasingly important, which must realize the responsibility before society in the formation of values, in positioning of education and knowledge. With this revision of values, the departure from a cult of consumption that was dictated by the market is important. It wasn't in vain that some analysts determined our epoch as the time of escapist and burdensome excess of information, obligated propaganda, commercial and entertainment—a burden that was imposed by consumption of information, for which the mass media bears considerable responsibility.

Currently, the importance of changing values is more and more recognized, which are determined on a fundamental level, the development of society, human behavior and the formation of his personality. Some rely on the church, which was traditionally the keeper of moral norms, and assert them in the social mind.

However, in modern society the role of the mass media in the formation of values is very great. In his day, Christ banished the tradesmen from the temple. Isn't it time to do the same thing with television, as well? All the more so given that today, people spend more time in front of their television screens than in front of an altar.

> *"Christ banished the tradesmen from the temple. Isn't it time to banish them from our television screens as well?"*

The Internet became a completely new informational phenomenon. Its appearance and headlong expansion became a new factor in the informational development of humanity, the meaning of which has only just begun to be realized.

The Internet led to the appearance of the global connection and informational system, in essence having realized the idea of an interacting society, which long since occupied the minds and imaginations of thinkers of the past. Today this has become reality, and a mass of questions have sprung up before a confused humanity.

The author's goal is not to examine the Internet as a major, new factor in the informational development of humanity. However, its appearance provides powerful confirmation of the informational nature of humanity, which in full measure defined its development in the past, and now, having become the dominant power, can show limited influence on the growth and development of humanity as well.

On the one hand, back in 1965, the prominent Soviet psychologist A.N. Leont'ev[46] shrewdly observed that "a surplus of information leads to poverty of the soul." I would have wanted to see these words on every site on the Web. But, on the other hand, what qualitative shifts in our social evolution will follow after the total informational revolution has overtaken humanity? This question is only just put forth; however, it undoubtedly will demand a new understanding and a new approach to assessing the deeper consequences of information and the demographic revolution.

From this stems the conclusion regarding the priorities of the development of humanity—about its transfer in the field of inner use of intellectual resources, programming – 'software,' and not 'hardware,' to use computer analogies. Behind this naturally follow considerable strategic and practical conclusions about the priorities of development and stability of the global system of agriculture itself, when the informational superstructure of an economy's administration, secured by the development of culture and science, is put to the fore.

Everything for the most part comes down to the problem of the choice of goals, and administration becomes the center in the development of humanity, when it would have been naïve to suppose that the invisible hand of self-organization would lead us to an unknown goal. For this, there is a catastrophic shortage of time, and it is the scarcest resource of humanity in the years of global reorganization by an intense current crisis and rapidly growing contradictions.

Finally, it is impossible to solve the problem of development in the society of knowledge without a global base in the form of fundamental science. Since growth is limited by the resources of human consciousness, and not material resources in the form of nourishment, energy and space, specifically knowledge and the understanding of it, increasingly becomes a factor that defines our development by entrance into the global community.

We see how global demographic transition limits growth in developed countries and this occurs because of internal processes and shows, in the first place, a sharp decrease in the number of children per female. In the

---

[46] Alexei Nikolaevich Leont'ev was a Soviet developmental psychologist, and the founder of activity theory.

near future this question will inevitably arise before developing countries as well, which are already enveloped by the global demographic revolution. Furthermore, we see that up to now there is no sufficient understanding of the situation, which arose at the time when these demographic processes are unfolding very quickly. It is specifically this that forces us to turn our attention towards the questions which are bound to the loss of tempos of reproduction of the population.

The voices of those who propose in the future to limit the growth of population of our planet, originating from exhaustion of natural resources, are heard louder and louder. However, calculated rates show that resources are fully sufficient for a population of 10–20 billion [18]. Hence there is every reason to examine the connection between the crisis of reproduction and the global demographic revolution.

In conclusion, the following is emphasized: under global analysis in the first approach, growth and development are not limited by energy and other resources and natural environment, but this does not mean that the given factors can be fully neglected. Their record is possible in the second approach, which should be based on a model of growth of humanity with the calculation of development of the global economy and the problem of the distribution of resources.

"Assessments show that based on the availability of natural resources, a population of 10–20 billion is completely acceptable."

Stability of Growth and System-Defined Crisis

Our analysis leads to an unambiguous conclusion about the reason for global demographic transition, which is connected to the achievement of the demographic system of the limit of the speed of growth and population of the world, occurring in the regime with intensification. This conclusion is essential, since it denies the Malthusian population principal, according to which resources are the limiting factor of growth. However, in the epoch of rapid changes, when their time becomes commensurable with the time of the life span of a person, a question arises about the stability of the process of growth and development.

The world wars of the 20th century were the most grandiose global catastrophes in the history of humanity, when in the course of two generations a decrease in the population of 8–10% took place (Figure 8). Then, on the eve of the war in 1913, the economies of Russia and Germany were growing by 10% a year and Russia's population was growing by 2% a year, and, due to these high tempos, the reason for the loss of political and economic stability in Europe could be seen. Therefore there are grounds for looking at the world wars of the 20th century as the result of the loss of the system stability of growth, no matter how mechanical this sounds. Indeed, according to Lyapunov's[47] criteria, maximum instability should be expected close to the beginning of the world demographic transition.

An influential mind of the 20th century and a participant in the peace negotiations at Versailles, English economist John Maynard Keynes[48] [50], in his instructive book *The Economic Consequences of Versailles' World* in 1920, primarily pointed to the role of demographic factors in the destabilization of the world on the eve of the First World War:

> Before the war the total population of Germany and Austria-Hungary not only exceeded the quantity of the population of the United States, but was practically equal to the entire population of the North American continent. Specifically in this quantity of the population, the occupied compact territory contained the might of the central powers. But such population numbers (even the war did not noticeably decrease it[49]), if the people were to be deprived of the means of existence, would present a danger to the world in Europe[50]. The European part of Russia increased its population to an even

---

[47] Aleksandr Mikhailovich Lyapunov was a Russian mathematician, mechanic and physicist.

[48] John Maynard Keynes, 1sr Baron Keynes, CB, FBA was a British economist whose ideas have fundamentally affected the theory and practice of modern macroeconomics, and informed the economic policies of governments.

[49] German general losses by the end of 1918 as a result of decrease of birthrate and increase of mortality in comparison to 1914 are assessed at 2.7 million people.

[50] The position, because of which, Keynes was not agreeing with British delegation and hence why he resigned. The history showed the entire rightfulness of his judgment. – *Author's note.*

greater extent than Germany—from less than 100 million in 1890 to 150 million at the start of the war[51].

In the year immediately preceding 1914, the excess of births over deaths in Russia as a whole was impressive—more than 2 million a year. This unusually rash growth in the Russian population, to which in England they did not pay proper attention, nevertheless became one of the most essential factors of recent years. Grand events of history are often obliged to slow a century-long path of population growth, which because of its progressive nature slips away from the attention of modern observers and hence is added to the weaknesses of government officials or the fanaticism of atheists.

The extraordinary events that occurred in the past two years in Russia—the greatest upheaval of society, having overturned that which seemed so stable, religion; the foundation of property and land-ownership; and also the forms of government organization and hierarchy of classes— could be more obliged to the deep influence of the increasing quantity of the population, than Lenin or Nicholas; excess fertility could have played a greater role in the destruction of persistency of society, than the strength of ideas or mistake of autocracy [40].

In such a way, the fast growth in the early stage of demographic transition is connected with the potential instability of the demographic system and this possibility should be considered by analysis of the stability of growth in the recent past and foreseeable future.

It's impossible not to recall how close to the loss of stability the world came in the years of the Cold War. A monstrous number of weapons of mass destruction had accumulated—close to 30,000 nuclear warheads on each side. For every inhabitant of the planet three tons of explosives fell, and the climatic consequences of a large nuclear war would have been apocalyptic in our days. Strategic arming was created for the purposes of mutual containment—a state of virtual war.

However, a confrontation between two systems could not have threatened stability, and there was always the likelihood of breakdown, when even the smallest indignation could have led to large and even

---

[51] Including Poland and Finland, but excluding Siberia, Central Asia and Caucasus

catastrophic global consequences. It has happened this way from the time of the First World War, the course of which was very far from the plans of all the generals and their headquarters. This is exactly why the recently concluded agreement on strategic arms reduction between the RF (Russian Federation) and the USA is so important, and the way out from nuclear confrontation between the great powers and decreased the possibility of accidental exchange of nuclear strikes was found.

Knowing the natural laws of growth of Earth's population, the losses of humanity during the time of the First and Second World Wars of the 20th century can be assessed. For this, the decrease in the world's population from 1914 to 1975 should be summarized, which comes out to about 11 billion people of x years. If we accept 45 years for an effective age, then integral losses of the population will amount to 250 billion people or 17,000 people a day on average! At the same time the population of the world grew from 1.8 billion in 1914 to 4.1 billion by 1975 and, amazingly, returned to the initial trajectory, demonstrating the unusual stability of the hyperbolic growth of humanity. At the time of the demographic recession of 1914–1950, the financial crisis of 1929 took place. But, against the backdrop of population losses due to world wars, to underscore demographic losses, connected essentially with economic recession, would have been difficult.

However, from 1980, as a result of the demographic revolution, a departure from the hyperbolic trajectory of growth begins, by which humanity invariably developed over the course of millions of years; then, as in 2011, explosive self-similar growth could have led to the world's population being 10 billion instead of 7 billion, which is what we see in reality.

It should be noted that for the USA, the mobilization of the economy that was generated by the Second World War promoted overcoming the consequences of the economic depression. In 1987 a memorable (for me) meeting took place with the eminent American economist John Galbraith[52], who directed the USA's war economy when Roosevelt gave him 'dictatorial authority'; he described this by saying: "I became the tsar of the economy." However, right after the victory, this centralized system of leadership was dismantled and Galbraith said with regret, "In our country

---

[52] John Kenneth Galbraith was a Canadian and later U.S. economist, public official and diplomat, and a leading proponent of 20th century American liberalism.

this did not happen." It required 50 more years for such *restructuring* and the non-mobilization of the economy, the ghost of which still haunts us.

> *"In the boundaries of the meetings with American economists, a conversation with Milton Friedman[53] stuck in my memory. He was more interested in the events in Russia, and his main observation was, 'You have a big country with different social conditions and a different economy. Therefore, do not hasten with your reforms.' This he repeated like a refrain in the year of Gaidar's 'shock therapy.'"*

We note in conclusion that in defiance of all liberal dogma, the first reaction to the financial economic crisis became the direct intervention of the US government in the economy. One of the decisions was the bailout of General Motors—not in vain, as it is well known, that what is good for GM is good for the USA!

In our time the management of society and its social and economic growth came once again into contradiction. This disparity between administration and growth, in essence, led to a severe crisis in the global financial system in 2008, which was systematic in nature. Already in 2006, the author noted:

> *Near the border of stability, small upheavals intensify, before the system loses stability. In the system, enveloped by strong connections, analogous to the global financial market, virtual money, similar to reactive power in electric networks, circulating in the system, significantly more than those that are invested. Large fluctuations in financial systems point out that the system is found close to the border of its stability. The introduction of a small tax on these useless operations, proposed by Tobin, could have called fading and stabilization of the system, which, however, seems unlikely, despite the fact that the global speculative financial pyramid moves toward the large crisis [3, pg. 164].*

---

[53] Milton Friedman was an American economist, statistician, and writer who taught at the University of Chicago for more than three decades.

This observation is based on considerations related to the stability of complex network systems. Whether the current crisis will lead to a profound disruption of the economy, to the decline of production and mass unemployment or even political collapse, still it remains to be seen. Primarily, for individual countries, the development of the crisis could lead to a further decrease in the birthrate and reduction of life expectancy. However, the collective analysis of the stability of development of the global demographic system indicates that possibly the maximum global instability of development has already passed.

Thus, it could be assumed that the upcoming epoch of stabilization of the world's population with a new structure of time will be sustainable. In this epoch, the appearance of new development goals should be expected, striving for quality of life instead of the quantitative growth which dominated before.

To such unexpected results and to the conclusion that the resources as a whole do not confine growth, could have only come from an overall analysis of the dynamic model. Therefore, this is why the assessment of the prominent historian, V.S. Myasnikov, was so essential for the author; it contains an in-depth analysis of the basic tenets of the theories—it was no wonder he called the review *The Russian anti-Malthus* [11]. In the future, insofar as the long-term stabilization of the population and a fundamental change in the historical process can be expected, the demilitarization of the world, with a decrease in the demographic factor in global strategic tension and a new temporal periodization of global history.

The scale of the problem, undoubtedly, demands a more detailed examination of the alternatives for development on the basis of complex interdisciplinary and international research program of our future. At this time it should be expected that in the foreseeable future, the economic and political center of Eurasia and the world will be more connected with the East, first of all, with China and India. Europe will remain an asset because of its past might, cultural and scientific potential. And finally, one last remark: will the upheavals, caused by demographic revolution, lead to the appearance of totally unexpected forms of development and new actors on the global stage? One way or another, the fundamental reorganization not only of man's consciousness and society, but, possibly, in the long run, of the nature of man himself, is inevitable.

Russia in the Global Context

President V.V. Putin, in an address to the Federal Assembly in 2006, singled out the most important problems facing Russia. In first place, the President mentioned the crisis of the birth rate, having concluded that, at that time, each woman in the country had an average of 1.3 children—nearly one less than the required average. At such a level, the birth rate of the country could not have even maintained the quantity of the population, which in the modern time in Russia has fallen by 2 million people over 10 years [33].

But, as we saw, a small birthrate today is characteristic of all developed countries, which can be examined as the consequence of demographic transition itself. In Russia, the maternal capital favored births in the families of a second child, since in these processes in Russia play a considerable role due to material factors because of strong and growing material stratification of society. However, as it should be from the world experience, proposed measures, and material benefit including, can only partially fix the high degree of instability in distribution of incomes in our country, threatening the condition of crisis already of its safety and integrity. Finally, the fundamental and even main role belongs to the moral crisis in the modern developed world—a crisis of the system of values.

In reference to Russia's demographic problems, the significance of detailed and systematic research into the country's human potential in the analytical note *Russia before the Face of Demographic Challenges,* written by a group of authors under the editorship of A.G. Vishnevskiy and S.N. Bobilev [32, 33] has been noted. Completed within the framework of the United Nations Development Program UNDP, the report is a contribution to the the global network of the UN in the field of development, prominent for positive changes in the life of people by providing the country-participants to the sources of knowledge, experience and resources.

The most serious danger for individual countries, as well as for Russia, was the growing economic inequality. The problem of inequality, which should be examined as a global event, is connected with the mechanism of quadratic growth itself. Unlike quasi-balanced growth, at which of the reverse mechanism of the market promoted a decrease in economic gradients, at the collective mechanism of growth these gradients intensify.

The same occurs in the regime of the monopoly, when compensated market processes are depressed.

Econometric analysis of processes in the framework of the program of Russia's demographic development is also given by A. U. Shchevyakov [34]. He himself undertook research into the economic inequality in Russia, which is not only not diminishing, but, paradoxically, increased during the course of the socio-economic crisis. As a result, inequality turned into one of the most intense problems, threatening the stability of our society and the integrity of the state. At present, the population of Russia is falling

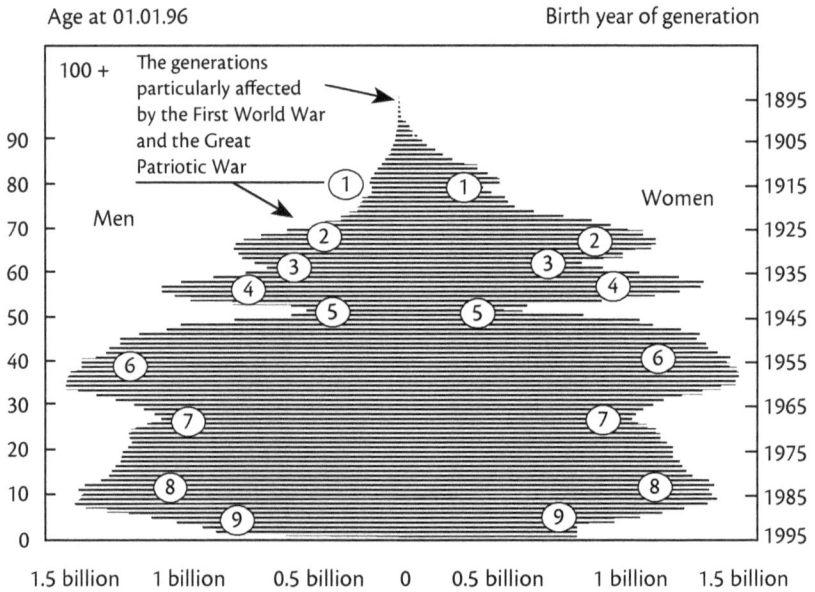

Figure 16. Age pyramid for Russia for 1995

1 – fall in the birth rate during the First World War and the Civil War; 2 – compensatory increase in the birth rate after the Civil War; 3 – collectivization, dekulakization (1928) and famine 1933; 4 – prohibition of abortions in 1936 and Natalisticheskaya policy; 5 – fall in the birth rate during the Great Patriotic War; 6 – growth in the birth rate after the war and during the 'thaw' under Khrushchev; 7 – demographic echo of the Great Patriotic War; 8 – the new family policy and the rise in the birth rate under Gorbachev; 9 – the current fall in the birth rate and the second echo of the war [2]

by 200,000 people each year, and by the time of the census of 2010 it had fallen by 1.4 million to 142 million relative to the census of 2002.

Unfortunately, in Russia, in the absence of the state approach and long-term plans and goals of quality education, and especially the politics in relation to the mass media, leads to the intensification of the crisis of self-consciousness and increases the further atomization and disintegration of society. Furthermore, we completely thoughtlessly import and even spread the views, only reinforcing the split of the family and breaking the link between generations, contributing to the worsening of the demographic situation in Russia.

Figures 16 and 17 show how, over 30 years—from 1980 to 2010 – the birth rate and the mortality rate changed in Russia. The graph is interesting in that it clearly shows the dependence of the most important demographic characteristics of the population from occurring in the country of social changes, connected with the passing of the demographic transition.

In the first half of the 1990s, more specifically in 1992, the graphs of birth rates and death rates crossed; at this point the first of them continued

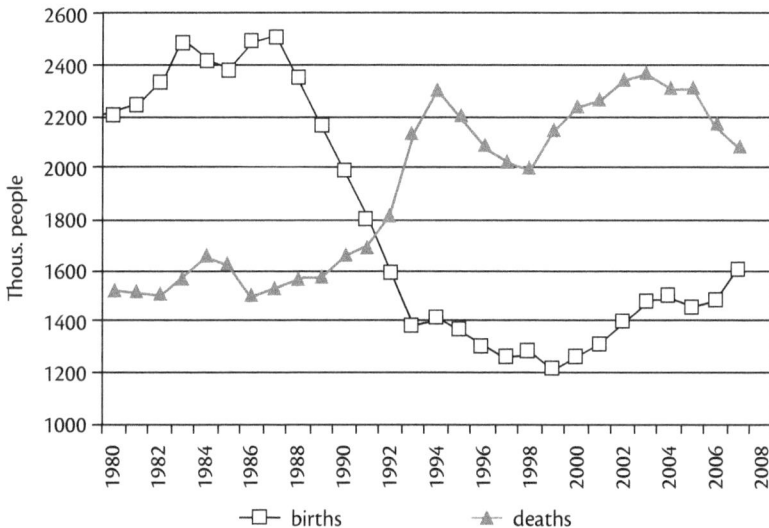

Figure 17. The 'Russian cross' – the number of births and deaths of Russian citizens over the past 30 years [33]

to drop and the second—to rise. This phenomenon was given the name of the 'Russian Cross' (Figure 17). The appearance of this 'cross' meant that the natural growth of the Russian population became negative. Pure migration that increased the population of Russia started to decline. This trend remains to this day. Now the 'solution' to the cross is decreasing and the main reason for this is temporarily favorable age-specific correlations in the population of Russia. However, the situation will soon change, hence to reverse the trend of the Russian Cross (though a 'cross' such as this is typical for many other countries, such as Hungary, Germany, Latvia, Ukraine, etc.) in the foreseeable future is unlikely, especially since the financial crisis will only strengthen these processes in the change of duration of life.

A considerable factor for Russia became migration, which gives up to half the growth of the population's quantity. With the return of Russians to the motherland, the country receives the people, enriched with the experience of other cultures. No less important is the inflow of economic immigrants from contiguous countries, which in general boosts the working class. Migration has become a new and very dynamic event in the demographics of Russia, and presents problems of its own. It could only be noted that in the Russian context many of them possess a character that is similar to that of other countries. Thus, substitution of fundamental ethnicities with new ones which, as a rule, are more prolific, is taking place [33, 46].

Of all the developed countries, Russia is distinguished by a high death rate among men. For them, the average life span is 59 years—practically 20 years less than the USA or Japan. Furthermore, the duration of life of men in Russia decreased 4 times compared to that of China [54]. The reason is the sorry state of the public health system, which undoubtedly exacerbates the thoughtless monetary approach to organization of this field of social protection of citizens, and also in the extremely inadequate pension provisions.

From the improvement of the economic situation until the beginning of the economic crisis, an increase in the duration of life has been observed. However, the crisis and growing unemployment, especially in the provinces, may slow down these positive trends. Thus, even now, during a time of crisis, there has been a marked increase in the number of abortions.

The consequence of the above-mentioned processes has been the breakup of the family; catastrophic for Russian history is the growth of the number of homeless children, which has achieved epidemic proportions. The reduction of the role of moral factors and the value of human life in the social conscience is also occurring due to this, which is what Robert Rozhdestvensky[54] wrote about [55]:

> *In the search of happiness, work, citizenship*
> *A strange custom*
> > *Appeared in Russia:*
>
> *Children*
> *Are fed up of being born to us—*
> *They believe we will manage just fine*
> *Without them.*

These processes are followed by a rise in alcoholism and suicides, the impossibility of self-fulfillment and the hardships of adapting to the new socio-economic conditions of growing unemployment, intensified upon the approach of financial crisis and the downturn in industry. In the modern world it is harder and harder for people to manage stress, or to live through the extreme conditions of modern life, primarily those of post-war syndrome, be it Vietnam, Iraq, Afghanistan or Chechnya. This is why waging a 'small victorious war' is so expensive—history offers us many examples of this. However, in a situation of growing crisis, the presence of nuclear weapons in a larger number of countries and the possibilities of a 'major war' cannot be excluded.

Symptomatic events are taking place with the language. With the fall of empires and detachment of national education, languages become instruments of nationalism. On the other hand, as a result of migration and globalization, the language gets congested with foreign words—slang. The decline in consciousness leads to the penetration of obscene language, and the wedge-like speech patterns of SMS texting, into the language.

---

[54] Robert Ivanovich Rozhdestvensky was a Soviet poet who broke with socialist realism in the 1950s-1960s along with such poets as Andrei Voznesensky, Yevgeny Yevtushenko and Bella Akhmadulina

It could be argued whether or not to assess these as the symptoms of crisis or whether we are witnessing the 'normal' evolution of language. Here is an essential and social position of the intelligentsia, which, having received freedom, imagined that this also liberates it from responsibility before society at the critical moment of the history of our country and the world, when, in the ideological vacuum, humanity is earnestly awaiting the answer to eternal questions about the meaning and value of our life…

"The intelligentsia, having received freedom, imagined that it was also free from responsibility before society."

General Positions and Conclusions

Here the results of our analysis have been brought together.
- From the moment when, 5–7 million years ago, a mutation of the gene HAR1 F, responsible for the growth of the brain, took place, humanity developed as a whole system, as a population of one type – *Homo*. A new quality of consciousness led to the passing and multiplication of information to a new global mechanism of development.
- Collective information interaction in the course of the last 1.6 million years determined the growth and social evolution of humanity. As a result, its quantity increased 100,000 times in comparison with the population of animals similar to humans in size and natural habitat, such as bears, wolves or large monkeys, not gifted in full measure by language and consciousness.
- This interaction, proportional to the square of the population of Earth, leads to hyperbolic growth that is headed into infinity starting from 2020. Such interaction is not linear, is not local and on average brings memory into the equation of growth. Contradiction is the

result of an unstable and unequal growth increase by the measure of development of the demographic crisis.

- The global quadratic growth, determined in 'large form', is stable. To this point, exponentially decreasing cycles of development are in complete accord with that periodicity, which is established by historians and anthropologists. However, the development in 'small form' is limited in space and time, is unstable and displays all the signs of dynamic chaos.

- The flow of historical time turns out to be unstable, speeding up in the regime with intensification as far as the approach to the time of demographic revolution. Since humanity cannot further support the increase of the speed of growth, a phase of transition begins and growth stops. Thus a fundamental reconstruction of the regime of development of humanity and a transition to a constant population of the world ~10 billion takes place.

- Transition occurs thanks to inward processes of the kinetics of growth, which are determined by the duration of reproductive growth—about 45 years. Exhaustion of resources or a change in the surrounding environment, all of the importance of these factors, are not determining. Specifically, inner systematic factors, conditioned by development, must be the focus of attention of the world and national political circles and crucially accounted for in decisions regarding the management of the development of society.

Such a fundamental shift in the paradigm of development in the critical time of global changes provides a deep influence on all aspects of the life of humanity, increasing the significance of the quality of humanity and society instead of the quantitative criteria which dominated in the recent past.

"The stabilization of the population of our planet was the result of the global crisis of growth of the population and development of the economy, when old ideas and slogans lost their meaning and the ability to inspire the people of the world."

Conclusion

Research and discussion of the global demographic process led to the discovery of the informational nature of the mechanism of growth and expansion of our views about the entire development of humanity, including the present. The conclusion that humanity, on the path of unchangeable hyperbolic growth as a whole, disposed of the required resources and energy, without which it would have been impossible to reach the present level of development, is considerable. Due to this, the growing potential of productive powers supplied the growth, but principally did not limit it, as this was proposed in Malthus's models.

The problem does not consist in the limit of resources, or in the global lack of energy, but in social mechanisms of management and distribution of knowledge, wealth and land, which is especially sharply evident in Russia. Indeed, how this follows from the model, in the world exist regional overpopulations and evident poorness, poverty and hunger, but these are local aspects and not the result of a global lack of resources.

Compare India and Argentina: the area of Argentina is 30% less than the area of India, the population of which is almost 30 times larger. However, with their own resources, the Argentines could produce enough food to feed the entire world. At the same time, in India, the production of agriculture is such that the gathered harvest in other years is twice as great as demand. Nevertheless, in a number of cases, provinces are starving, since there is no effective system of food distribution and storage.

In the world, enveloped by globalization, the problems of food, public health and education, energy and ecology demand the development of concrete political recommendations, on which depend the development and safety of countries and the world as a whole. After all, in the modern world, the producing powers reached such a level that in order to support the life of humanity, 15–20% of its working power is enough. Therefore a redistribution of the priorities of development is taking place, and culture and science, in all their manifestations, and the problem of employment, acquire more meaning.

In this field, Russia, thanks to its traditions in the system of education, has now made a considerable start; however, it remains fundamentally behind in the development and effectiveness, such as in agriculture and industry. From that, our future depends on how successfully it can overcome this disparity. This will determine the place our country is going to take in the global world, including the role that lies in store for it in the fate of the contiguous countries, after which Russia is freed from the obligations of the past. This is why in the post-Soviet space, as in Europe, economic integration of countries can be foreseen, which will be followed by interaction in the field of education and culture; there will be no prospects for development in this region.

In the time of the Great Economic Depression of 1929, Canes, addressing his grandchildren, wrote:

> Let's imagine that in a hundred years we will be eight times richer than to-day... If one assumes that there will be no large wars or considerable growth of the population, then the economic problem will be resolved... This means that the economic problem is not, if we would look into the future, a relentless concern of humanity.
>
> Why, you should ask, is it so strange? This amazes me because if we would refer to the past, then we would discover that the economy is the fight for survival, was not only a vital task of humanity, but was such for the entire tsardom of the living from that time, when life in its most primitive forms appeared. From the very beginning we have evolved in nature with all our aspirations and deep instincts for the decision of economic tasks. If the economic problems will be solved, then humanity will be deprived of its first-born goal. This is why I, with horror, think about how one should redirect habits and instincts of the common human, which have been assembled in his consciousness over the course of many generations and from which we now ask to refuse in a few decades. To express myself in modern language, should we not anticipate a "nervous breakdown?"
>
> Hence, from the first moment of his appearance, the human stands before an appeal: how to use the freedom from vital economic questions, how to occupy the spare time, which was conquered for him by science and growing income, to live wisely, in harmony and peace...
>
> There will be other changes in other fields, which undoubtedly will come, when the accumulation of wealth will cease to be socially significant, deep changes will happen in moral arrangements as well. We will be able to discard many pseudo moral principles, which pursued us over the course

of two hundred years, when we erected some of the most abominable characteristics of human nature in rank of the highest virtues. The thirst for money as the means of accumulating, as opposed to the method of reaching for happiness and goals in life, will be viewed as that, which in reality it is—as an unhealthy passion. As one of those semi-criminal and semi-pathological inclinations, the shuddering study of which should be left to the specialist in emotional illnesses.

However, don't be too hasty! The time has not passed yet. We must still pretend for a hundred more years that black is white and white is black, after all, in meanness there is benefit, and in nobility—there is none. Therefore, money-lending, greed and prudence for now still remain our deities [41].

This incredible prophesy comes to mind today, when the foresight of Canes becomes reality—that future, which already came. Production of energy already reached the level that was pointed out by Canes. Hence many of the above-viewed consequences of the demographic revolution serve as confirmation of the foresight of this great economist, who did much for the overcoming of the economic crisis of 1929, and we refer once more to his inheritance and ideas about the roles of states in managing the economy. It could be that the most essential is that the problems of personal values and goals of humanity stood in front of us in their entire magnitude.

Analysis of the quantitative growth of the population allows us to describe the total result of all economic, social and cultural industry of humans, which at first opens the way to a collective understanding of history. The main result of the experience of fundamental research into the development of humanity and its consequences in the foreseeable future, where the temporal scale of existence determines the transition from chaos to management consists in this.

This approach led to the necessity of transformation of the understanding of time in history, when the time and development turn out to be a coupled variable. Hence why, in the given work, the central place is given over to the global kinetics of the quantitative growth of humanity and the principal of demographic imperative—those views, to which we refer during the explanation of processes in history, demography and economy on the basis of the collective theory of growth.

In other words, the proposed method gives us a rough skeleton of collective views about the development of humanity. However, in the future, the bones have to accumulate tissue and muscles, finally finding room for the soul and thoughts, and with this, to fully imagine the figure of humanity. In this one would have wanted to hope for understanding and cooperation with public sciences. Hence the stated approach should be developed in social sciences, just as in public consciousness. After all, the discourse is about the theory of humanity as a whole, and about the circumstances of our life that are closest to us.

The approach developed here becomes a natural step to description and foresight, and consequently, to active management of the future, in which, in the society of knowledge, a leading role is played by culture and science. The author understands the contradictions arising in this case, with many generally accepted views; however, his goal was possibly a more full clarification of the mechanism of development, which is obliged to collective interaction. It is based on the potential of our mind on both the individual, and the societal level, and expressed in public consciousness, in culture. It is this in particular that separates us from animals, with their instincts, and is realized in society through upbringing and education.

The new approach to global problems must rely on cooperation of scientists, in the possession of necessary intellectual potential that belongs to different traditions and different social experiences. Searching for a new synthesis as the foundation of new politic, primarily, should revive traditions of interdisciplinary researchers in Russian science. The answer to this clear social order became the organization of the Department of Global Problems in the Russian Academy of Sciences and respective faculty in Moscow State University.

In connection with the necessity of development of global problems is the interesting remark of the President of the Royal Scientific Society of Great Britain, Lord Robert May:

> A question that is interesting to discuss is presented, whether or not the inhabitants of other planets are separated—if they exist—share our intellectual passion of the fate of the Universe and the construction of the atom, which mostly surpasses the interest of living creatures with whom we inhabit our world. Similar to this question are hardships which face managing

*organizations, when they must make the decisions for long-term problems
as opposed to short-range ones, such as climate change...*

*Such questions do not belong to solvable problems in that sense
that they were chosen by Medawar, determining the scientific problems
specifically as solvable. However, similar questions determine the future of
humanity, which thereby influence the fate of everything alive on Earth [53].*

The priority task of global science, systems of education and mass
media, including the UN and UNESCO, must become complex research on
an interdisciplinary foundation, with developed international cooperation
and propaganda of views about global problems. In such a case, a deeper
analysis of system processes and the expenditure of conceptual space must
become the basis of our understanding of the unique epoch of the greatest
crisis in the entire history of humanity. At this unavoidable point in history,
as well as the dynamic of growth of the population of Earth.

These processes are very impetuous, the changes occur in one or two
generations, unlike the slower changes of climate and ecology, which always seem to end up at the center of politicians' attention. Therefore, today, such social order from the future must meet the system of researchers, organization of science and education, primarily for upbringing of
the most able and responsible members of society, the manufacturing of
new views from science about society and comprehension of the modern
world.

In conclusion, we notice that the discussion of the most varied aspects
of history shows all manner of influences on the part of information
and knowledge on the development of humanity, which from the
very beginning and on its own level was an informational community.
However, the solutions to the problems of development and stability
of growth—globally, as on a national scale—are impossible without
coordination of effort, without the choice of target and political will. Thus,
for the achievement of economic effectiveness, stochastic and local market
mechanisms must be used. However, managing more meaningful processes
on the global scale demands a special approach. It is specifically this that
distinguishes global problems in comparison with all other questions,
attracting the attention of politicians and financiers, scientists of exact
science, historians and sociologists.

The same goes for cultivating the system of values, when we can foresee more active interference as a civic society, as the state in element of chaos and private interests, dominating in the mass media system. Of paramount importance for Russia is the preservation of traditions and development of our position in the system of education, which showed its own richness during the epoch of change. After all, education consists in understanding and not in the accumulation of knowledge, all the more so given that knowledge depreciates faster and faster.

In this case, science and culture increasingly move into the role of political factors, expressing the dictates of the demographic imperative in the global development of humanity. A significant factor is geopolitical space, where for Russia the Eurasian supercontinent serves as a natural arena. With the conservation of long-standing connections with Europe, for us, with calculation of the growing significance of the potential and traditions of China and India, the Eastern direction becomes a prioritized vector of development—it is not for nothing that our coat of arms is a double-headed eagle wearing a crown.

However, the measure of our influence and might must become culture and science. This is related to the hopes of Russia and has reasons for historical optimism over the exit out of the crisis, resulting from the epoch of global demographic revolution, which we ended up living through. Since "blessed is he, who visited this world in its decisive minutes!"

The history of humanity is similar to the fate of man, who, having lived through an impetuous youth, a time of adventures and searching, studied, took part in battles, got rich and eventually got married, started a family and found peace. This theme has existed in global literature since the times of Homer and the tales of *A Thousand and One Nights*, the writing of St. Augustine, Stendhal and Tolstoy: just as in nature, the individual's development mirrors the evolution of the species.

Only the future will show this, and waiting for it should not take long.

"It could be that humanity will now, after the dramatic times of growth and change, will come to its senses and calm down."

Appendix

A Mathematical Theory of Population Growth

The global population, $N(T)$, will be described by the function from time, T, determinant on the condition of the demographic system of the Earth. Then the parameter of order—the leading variable, subjugated all other transitioning—will become the full number of people, N.

In this close functional correlation, the distribution of the population across our planet is not accounted for, nor its economic and aging condition, nor racial and national structure. The process of growth also will be examined in a considerable interval time, T, – a large number of generations. In other words, we will be examining the average value of variables and average functions. By this, primarily, is deposited into equations of memory about the past, determined by a time averaged variable.

Such an allocation of the main variables N and T and their averages is characteristic of a system-based approach. It was developed in synergy and is the basis of symptomless methods, engineered for the solving of tasks of great complexity, appearing in the examination of systems with many levels of freedom. These variables, which present the all-important social factors of age and gender, education and development, income and etc., are being described by statistical distributions. Hence, when such multi-factorial problems are examined, it can be supposed that certain limits of system development are statistically stationary and hence happen to be dynamically self-similar. This strong assumption means that there remain invariable proportions between comparative changes of time and population.

The meaning of this fundamental hypothesis of scaling consists in what is stated as the relative constancy of the rate change of the system analogous to the principal of inertia. In the given case it can be shown that such self-similar growth must be described as the degree function without the characteristic parameter, such as the scale of time. Such processes possess scale invariance—scaling—analogous to the developed turbulence in the flow of liquid.

These ideas are less familiar to historians and sociologists; however, they must help in the expenditure of those figures (characters), by which we describe the historical process.

This book shows how the data on global demographics lead to the formula (1):

$$N = \frac{200 \cdot 10^9}{2025 - T} = \frac{C}{T_1 - T} \text{ billions.} \tag{1}$$

When referring to the formula (1), the task of the theory consists of the establishment of the limits of its application as close to singularity, when this function is directed to infinity, as in the remote past, when it decreases too slowly. In other words, asymptotic form is limited in the past by zero and by a pole in the current time.

To be able to describe the transition, the time, characterizing internal processes, determinate by the duration of a person's life and his reproductive activity—those factors, while passing through the demographic transition limiting speed of growth by the measure of approach to its limit should be taken into consideration. For this we should refer to expression for the speed of growth in dependency of time, differentiated (1):

$$\frac{dN}{dT} = \frac{C}{(T_1 - T)^2}, \tag{2}$$

and after (later) insert the divergent expression characteristic time, limiting speed of growth in this:

$$\frac{dN}{dT} = \frac{C}{(T_1 - T)^2 + \tau^2}. \qquad (3)$$

This maneuver may appear to be an arbitrary step. However, here we referred to the methods, which are developed for the regulation of divergence that has appeared in the singularity of growth. The received expression describes the singularity of the global demographic transition very well, hence, integrating (3), we will receive the expression for the description of the transition itself and possess a mature asymptotic form:

$$N = \frac{C}{\tau} \cot^{-1}\left(\frac{T_1 - T}{\tau}\right). \qquad (4)$$

Referencing the last data (givens) of demographics (Figure 18) were received specified meanings of constants that are accounted for in all of the calculations:

$$C = 163 \text{ billion}, T_1 = \text{the year } 1995, \tau = 45 \text{ years}$$

and the extendable number $K = \sqrt{C/\tau} = 60\,000;$ (5)

$$\ln K = 11.00.$$

Due to the introduction of the final 'τ' pole in T_1, T_1 shifts to the new value of $T_1 = 1995$, which is indeed adopted in calculations describing both demographic transition and global population growth beyond the limits of T_1 as expressed in (4) (see Table 1).

In the recent past the expression, (4), asymptotically outright transitioned into an auto-model hyperbolic growth (1). However, applied to the very distant past, the speed of the growth must be limited from below. This proposal is enough so as to add linear growth to the remote past, at which in the first approximation, the speed of growth cannot be less than the appearance of one hominid through time τ, until the quantity of population reaches ~100000. In population genetics, the number K is characteristic for the quantity of stable number of species, biologically similar to man. At the achievement of this level in the quantity of species ~1.6 million years ago, the epoch of quadratic growth begins, which becomes dominant until the moment of demographic transition.

The parameter of K defines not only the scale of the quantity of humanity in the initial epoch of growth, but also gives the assessment of the quantity of a coherent group of people or tribe as a self-sufficient unit of the population.

As a large parameter, constant K defines all correlations between population and duration of processes of growth, and the considerable height of constant K leads to high effectiveness of asymptotic decisions. As a result of the speed of growth, the population of the Earth is defined by a nonlinear differential equation:

$$\frac{dN}{dt} = \frac{N^2}{K^2}, \tag{6}$$

where time $t = T/\tau$ is defined in units of time τ and in the solutions of the equation (6) counting from the moment of passing through demographic transition. Characteristic time τ is the same for phase transitions in the past and present.

The formula of growth (6) expresses the nature of the collective nonlinear interaction, which is responsible for the growth of humanity in the epoch of its explosive development between two singularities. In this equation T_1 and N for averaged variables and speed of growth is equal to development, which is equal to the quantity of the population of the world, as the expression of the measure of systematic complexity of the population of the planet.

The full decision must describe the growth of humanity in the course of three epochs. The first epoch, A – anthropogenesis begins from the linear growth with the above-designated minimal speed. When the population reaches the magnitude of about 100,000, epoch B begins—explosive growth with a growth rate proportional to the square of the population of Earth, and from this time, humans populate the entire planet.

When the speed of quadratic growth reaches its limit at double over characteristic time, τ, the crisis of universal demographic growth transitions into epoch C, where the stabilization of the population of the world takes place. Thus, on the basis (3), the maximum absolute speed of global growth at the time of demographic transition equals:

$$\left(\frac{dN}{dT}\right)_1 = \frac{K^2}{\tau} = 80 \text{ million a year} \qquad (7)$$

at a relative growth of:

$$\left(\frac{dN}{NdT}\right)_1 = \frac{2}{\pi\tau} = 1{,}40\% \text{ a year,} \qquad (8)$$

reached in 1995, which conform to the data of OON, but gives slightly less meaning for the absolute speed of growth at (by) comparison with Table 1 (Figure 18).

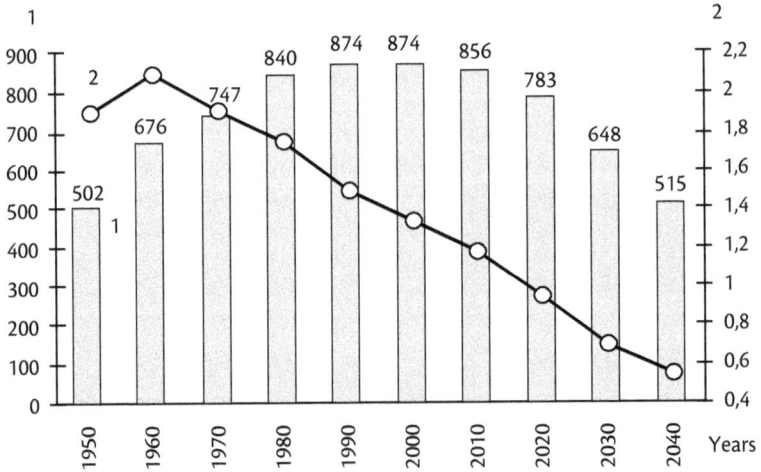

Figure 18. World demographic transition around the year 2000.

1 – absolute increase (growth) of population, averaged out per decade, in millions; **2** – relative increase, 1.40% per year (UN data)

Population of the Earth at this critical moment of transition $T_1 = 1995$ according to equal:

$$N_1 = \pi K^2/2 = 5680 \text{ million} \qquad (9)$$

On this foundation it is easy to determine the limit of, twice as big, then N_1, to which, in epoch C, asymptotically rushed the population of Earth:

$$N_\infty = 2N_1 = \pi K^2 = 11\ 360 \text{ million} \qquad (10)$$

In the context (within limits) of assumptions made, this number presents the higher assessment of the population of Earth in the foreseeable future. In such a manner, global interaction leads to an increased speed and synchronization of processes on the concluding stage of global demographic transition—to the narrowing of transition and thereby to the decreasing in the limit for population of our planet. This result agrees with the intuitive extrapolation made by demographers. The examination of $N(T)$ as an analytical function points to asymptotic behavior $T \to \infty$, when $N \to N_\infty$ there is an assumption of absence of zeros and pluses in the foreseeable future.

The beginning linear growth gives the assessment of time for the epoch of anthropogenesis and critical singularity in prehistory of humanity, which happened:

$$T_0 - T_1 = \pi/2 \cdot K\tau = -\tau \sqrt{\pi N_1/2} = 4{,}2 \text{ million years ago,} \quad (11)$$

if the known meaning for N_1 is used and the same meaning $\tau{=}45$ years for the singularity in the distant past and in the present. Despite simplifications made, given that the assessment fully conforms to the assessment of time, proposed for T_0 in anthropology.

This implies an interest in determining the total number of people living on Earth. If one imagines the variables in (6) and integrated:

$$P_{0,1} = \int_{t_0}^{t_1} N dt = K^2 \int_{K}^{K^2} \frac{dN}{N} = K^2 \ln K, \qquad (12)$$

then we will receive the number of people that lived from T_0 until our time T_1. In the assessments of other authors, the duration of a generation is accepted as the equal of 20 years, that leads to the assessment of $P_{0.1} = 106$ billion [10]. Hence it is necessary the insert (12) as the multiplier $45/20 = 2.25$:

$$P_{0,1} = 2.25 \ K^2 \ln K = 90 \text{ million.} \tag{13}$$

Thus, in the course of every, from $\ln K = 11.00$ allocated periods lived (by) $2.25K^2 = 8$ billion people. This number is invariant for number of people, living in exponentially declining cycles.

These cycles can be obtained, generalizing the solution (6) in the field of complex variables or summing up exponentially decreasing periods, at that the zero cycle $\theta = 0$ corresponds to linear growth in the course of the initial singularity:

$$\Delta T = K\tau \exp (-\theta), \tag{14}$$

where θ — number of the cycle, determining the duration of development at $K \gg 1$:

$$T_1 - T_0 = K\tau \sum_0^{\ln K} \exp(-\theta) =$$
$$= K\tau \left[\exp 0 + \exp(-1) + ... + \exp(-\ln K) \right] = \tag{15}$$
$$= \frac{e}{e-1} K\tau = 1{,}582 K\tau$$

and compare it with (11), where the duration is equal to:

$$T_1 - T_0 = \pi/2 \cdot K\tau = 1.571 \ K\tau$$

In (15) the growth is summed up by a hyperbolic trajectory, in the second case—by (4):

$$N = K \tan t / K$$

Demographic cycles determine the frequency of development of all of humanity for 4–5 million years, including progression along hyperbolic law the growth from the end of anthropogenesis until our days. The presence of demographic cycles, pointed out by anthropologists and historians, like epochs of development of humanity, points to global stability of the system at its development along (on) limited trajectory of hyperbolic growth.

For moving further, we will transition to changing $n = N/K$, when the population of Earth is measured in units K:

$$\frac{dn}{dt} = \frac{n^2 + 1}{K}, \qquad n = -\cot^{-1}\frac{t}{K}, \qquad (16a)$$

$$\frac{dn}{dt} = \frac{n^2}{K}, \qquad nt = -K, \qquad (16b)$$

$$\frac{dn}{dt} = \frac{K}{t^2 + 1}, \qquad n = -K\cot t, \qquad (16c)$$

$$\frac{dt}{dn} = \frac{t^2 + 1}{K}, \qquad t = -\cot^{-1}\frac{n}{K}, \qquad (16d)$$

Then the equations for growth become symmetrical and this is apparent by the coupling of the variables n and t. The change of the dependent variable in (16a) and (16d) occurs upon the passing of transition, when n becomes an independent variable instead of time t, which is expressed in equation of growth (3).

From (15) it follows that after every cycle, until demographic transition, there remains half of the time of duration of the cycle:

$$\frac{e}{e-1} - 1 = \frac{1}{e-1} = 0.583 \approx 1/2,$$

which is fully confirmed by the data of history and anthropology (Table 2).

The growth of the population can be illustrated by the geometric building of the function of tangent:

$$\tan\phi = \frac{AB}{OA} = \frac{N}{K} = n, \qquad (17)$$

where the angle reflects the flow of time, and an increase of population ΔN = 1 and N_0 = 1 (Figure 19).

The linear growth will continue until $\varphi_{A,B} = K\tau = 1$ and $N_B = \tan 1$ in the point B on tangent AC. Further growth $N = K\,(\pi/2 - \varphi)$ will pass along the hyperbola, at which the time it asymptotically approaches $\pi/2$ and the population will reach the meaning $N_C = \pi K^2/2$. When the system is approaching the moment of singularity, then from the equation (16a) should transition to the equation (16d), to describe the growth at the transition of singularity in the course of epoch C.

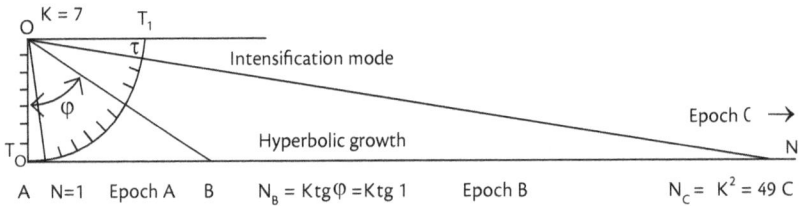

Figure 19. The construction of the function of a tangent, showing the limits of asymptotics of growth at K=7

The construction on Figure 19 shows that after the transition from linear to hyperbolic growth during epoch B there remains two times less time, then in the beginning epoch A. For the entire epoch B the time from T_0 to T_1 at $K=7$ is divided into 11 intervals. Since then $N_C = K^2 =$ 49 in the moment of intensification. However, even at such a small value of K, when $\ln 7 = 1.95$ gives good assessment $1 + \ln K3$ for the number of demographic cycles.

Thereby, the zero cycle A of anthropogenesis continued for 7 time units, the first cycle lasted 3 and the last – 1 unit of time. This construction shows how the discretion of time and population leads to the appearance of periodic growth, expressed in demographic cycles.

The linear growth describes the development of the system from the initial singularity of growth at N_0 = 1 and the positive meanings of N. Further follows the growth along the hyperbola and in the end—the singularity of demographic explosion. The construction, when variables N and T at passing in transition switch places, we leave to the reader.

Figure 20 shows functions that describe the growth of the system at $K = 1$, which appear in the construction of the solution, beginning with singularity in epoch A, transitioning afterwards in epoch B of hyperbolic growth and concluding with epoch C. Asymptotic transition of the solution, describing the growth in the beginning of development and in its final section, we will receive, referring to the rows for function $\cot^{-1}(t/K)$ and $\cot(t/K)$:

$$n = \cot^{-1} t/K = -\frac{K}{t}\left(1 - \frac{t^2}{3K^2} - \frac{t^4}{45K^2} - \dots\right), \quad t^2 \le \pi K^2 \qquad (18a)$$

$$n = \cot t/K = -\frac{K}{t}\left(1 - \frac{1}{3t^2} + \frac{1}{5t^4} - \dots\right), t^2 \ge 1 \qquad (18b)$$

These functions are intersecting at point A, in the middle at the logarithmic view between time T_0 and T_1, corresponding to the approach of neolith:

$$t_{1/2} = -\sqrt{K} \quad \text{and} \quad N_{1/2} = K\sqrt{K} \qquad (19)$$

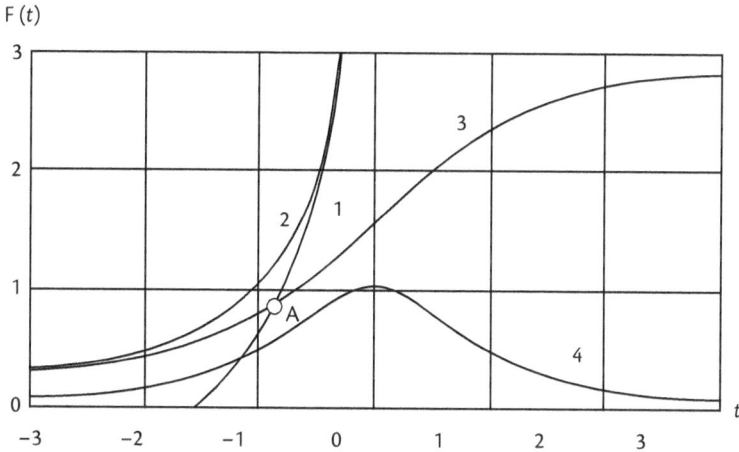

Figure 20. Function F(t), describing growth

$$1 - \cot t, \quad 2 - \frac{-1}{t}, \quad 3 - \cot^{-1} t \quad \text{and} \quad 4 - \frac{dn}{dt} = \frac{1}{t^2 + 1}.$$

under angle $2/(3K)$ and practically smoothly at $K \gg 1$.

It is obvious that the solution can be constructed, counting the time from T_0 – from the epoch of anthropogenesis A at $t_0 = 0$. Then, excluding t from (16c), having received one autonomous differential equation, describing the growth depending on the function of the system, which is determined by the population of Earth:

$$\frac{dn}{dt} = K \sin^2 \frac{n}{K} + \frac{1}{K} \qquad (20)$$

where the last term is added, such that the growth in the epoch A was never smaller of one hominid at $\Delta t = \tau$.

Having integrated (20) and for the values of $K > 1$ and of initial conditions $t_0 = n_0 = 0$, we will obtain the solution:

$$\tan \frac{n}{K} = \frac{1}{K} \tan \frac{t}{K} \qquad (21)$$

This equation shows the symmetry of variables N and T – population and time. For the development over the course of epoch B far from the singularities of growth, this is expressed in (16b) and follows from the complexity of casual connections in the frame of developed views of the nonlinear dynamic of the global system of the population of our planet.

So as to determine the stability of development, it follows to refer to the equation of the growth of humanity (20). On the basis of (15) in the linear approach, the stability of growth disturbance determines by Lyapunov's figure λ of development of instability in the system of population (Figure 21):

$$\delta N = \delta N_0 \exp(\lambda t)$$

$$\lambda = \frac{\partial}{\partial n}\left(\frac{dn}{dt}\right) = \sin\left(\frac{2n}{K}\right). \qquad (22)$$

According to the criteria when $\lambda > 0$ the movement until the transition is unstable and only after the transition, the development of the system becomes asymptotically stable and henceforth will remain so. A more

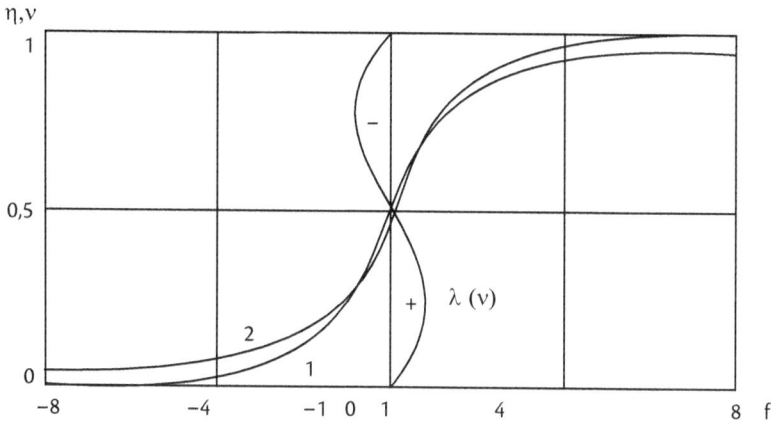

**Figure 21. The transitional processes and Lyapunov indicator $\lambda(\eta)$
for the stability of growth in the linear approach**

1 – logical transition, $\eta = 1/(1 + e^{-1} t)$;
2 – demographic transition $v = (1/\pi) \cot^{-1} t$

complete definition of stability will demand the insertion of distribution for N and referring to the methods of statistical physics in summarizing of the model.

During the hyperbolic growth, the immediate meaning of exponential growth is equal to antiquity:

$$T_E = \left[\frac{1}{N} \frac{dN}{dT} \right]^{-1} = T_1 - T, \qquad (23)$$

which defines the rate of processes of development in the moment of time T.

The complex issues, related to the limits of predictability of complex systems are reviewed in [56].

In hyperbolic chronology, the instant exponential scale of the time of growth and linear instability according to Lyapov depends on antiquity. Until the demographic transition, the instant value of time is equal to twice the time of growth of instability:

$$T_E = 2\tau\omega/\lambda$$

In the global system of the population of the world, it can be assumed that the distribution of the population of the cities and villages is described in degree law, possessing fractal nature [52]. In such case this distribution is well described by the expression:

$$U(R) = \frac{U_0 \ln U_0}{\ln U_0 + R},$$ (24)

where R – rank of the city, beginning with $R = 0$, and multiplier $\ln U_0$ is inserted for suppression of divergence at $R = 0$. Then the population of the largest city U_0 is defined by the decision of transcendental equation, connecting the population of the world N with U_0:

$$N = \int_{R_{\min}}^{R_{\max}} \frac{U_0 \ln U_0}{R + \ln U_0} = U_0 \ln^2 U_0 .$$ (25)

Refer to the examples: so, the population of Ancient Rome, where the Coliseum held 50,000 spectators, turns out to be equal to 1 million of the population of the world $N = 100$ million, which is consistent with the estimates of historians. On the other hand, the population of Peking at the end of the 17th century reached 3 million at the estimated population of the world equal to 700 million and estimates of demographers in 900 million. In 1985, with the population of the world 4.8 billion, the population of Tokyo, as the largest city, was equal to 17 million (Figure 22). In 2011, the world population is at 7 billion and the population of Tokyo, as the largest city, made up approximately 24 million (U_0 – 24 million). With the stabilization of the population of the Earth at $N_\infty = 11$ billion in the future, the population of the largest city will reach $U_\infty \sim 40$ million.

Taking into account the inaccuracy of the given demographics, agreement with these assessments is completely convincing. It serves as a confirmation that the population of the world is basically the system, enveloped by general interaction, leading to the mature fractal distribution of the population of the cities.

Along with the distribution of cities, it would be of interest to receive the distribution of means and resources for the entire population of the world. On such a graph, Pareto must be presented by everyone—from billionaires and oligarchs to bums and layabouts. Such distribution would

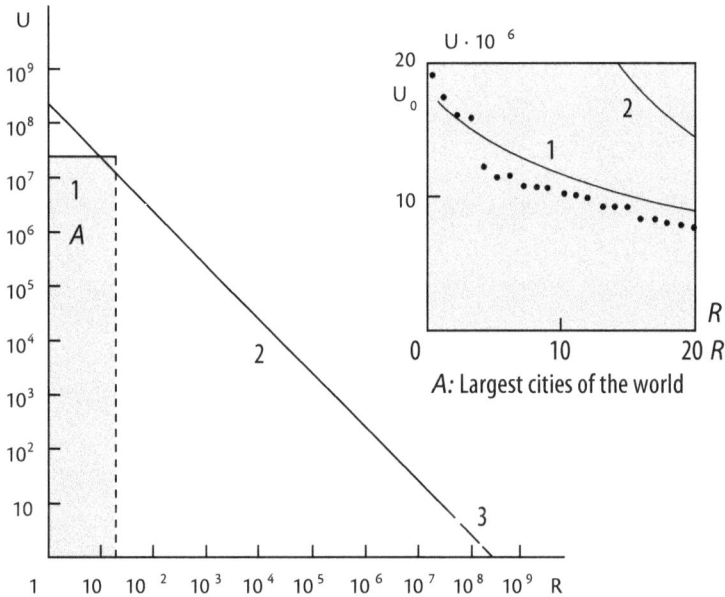

Inset A: The biggest cities in the world; R=0 – Tokyo; 1 – Mexico city; 2 – Tokyo; 3 – New York; 4 – Shanghai; 5 – Calcutta; 6 – Buenos Aires; 7 – Rio de Janeiro; 8 – London; 9 – Seoul; 10 – Mumbai; 11 – Los Angeles; 12 – Osaka; 13 – Beijing; 14 – Moscow; 15 – Paris; 16 – Jakarta; 17 – Tianjin; 18 – Cairo; 19 – Tehran; 20 – Delhi.

Figure 22. Distribution of world cities based on population.

have been given by the view about the unbalanced nature and evolution of the system of the global economy.

In the stated theory, the problem of the growth and development of all the world's population is viewed as a whole demographic system in the course of the entire history of humanity. Now, in this way, lasting more than a million years, the most important event of all meta-history is the global demographic revolution, which is now faced by the whole of humanity.

Such an approach to history and economy is of particular importance for Russia. It is specifically due to its geographical extent, the variety of climate conditions, ethnic mix, represented by fundamental global religions and a varied economy, that the global approach has such significance.

In order to understand the dynamics of growth and the self-organization of humanity, it is advisable to refer to the logarithmic reformed time of duration and examine the auto-model development in an asymptotic approach. In this approach resources do not influence global limitation of growth and its transition to stabilization of the population of the world is obliged to internal processes, expressed in the principle of demographic imperative.

Asymptotic solutions for nonlinear problems assume, as Ya. B. Zeldovich observed, the same value as private solutions to linear problems, where the principal of superposition operates. In our problem it is the auto-model solutions that have an asymptotic character, in which in some cases, independence from the parameter allows for equations in partial derivative to transition to ordinary differential equations. This occurs in problems about growth of humanity, when the nonlinear equation can neglect spatial distribution of the population, since in this approach the final movement of the Earth—migration of the population—does not influence the overall number of people.

The field of research into the theory of global population growth, undoubtedly, opens a wide field for head-on research into this problem, with a whole armory of modern methods of statistical physics, theory of phase transitions and the evolution of unstable systems. In essence, the proposed research is analogous to modern cosmology, to which many works on the fundamental problems of the organization of the world as a whole have been dedicated, visible and invisible. But a developed theory is much closer to us, since the problems relate to a much deeper understanding of the economy and history, which the exact sciences can, albeit presumptuously, propose.

Therefore, we express confidence that these problems will lead to the development of methods in theoretical physics and the creation of the basis for theoretical meta-history—the history of the growth and development of humanity as a whole.

Dear Reader,

Thank you for purchasing this book.

We at Glagoslav Publications are glad to welcome you, and hope that you find our books to be a source of knowledge and inspiration. We want to show the beauty and depth of the Slavic region to everyone looking to expand their horizon and learn something new about different cultures and different people, and we believe that with this book we have managed to do just that.

Now that you've gotten to know us, we want to get to know you. We value communication with our readers and want to hear from you! We offer several options:
– Join our Book Club on Goodreads, Library Thing and Shelfari, and receive special offers and information about our giveaways;
– Share your opinion about our books on Amazon, Barnes & Noble, Waterstones and other bookstores;
– Join us on Facebook and Twitter for updates on our publications and news about our authors;
– Visit our site www.glagoslav.com to check out our Catalogue and subscribe to our Newsletter.

Glagoslav Publications is getting ready to release a new collection and planning some interesting surprises — stay with us to find out more!

Glagoslav Publications
Office 36, 88-90 Hatton Garden
EC1N 8PN London, UK
Tel: + 44 (0) 20 32 86 99 82
Email: contact@glagoslav.com

Glagoslav Publications Catalogue

- The Time of Women by Elena Chizhova
- Sin by Zakhar Prilepin
- Hardly Ever Otherwise by Maria Matios
- Khatyn by Ales Adamovich
- Christened with Crosses by Eduard Kochergin
- The Vital Needs of the Dead by Igor Sakhnovsky
- A Poet and Bin Laden by Hamid Ismailov
- Kobzar by Taras Shevchenko
- White Shanghai by Elvira Baryakina
- The Stone Bridge by Alexander Terekhov
- King Stakh's Wild Hunt by Uladzimir Karatkevich
- Depeche Mode by Serhii Zhadan
- Herstories, An Anthology of New Ukrainian Women Prose Writers
- The Battle of the Sexes Russian Style by Nadezhda Ptushkina
- A Book Without Photographs by Sergey Shargunov
- Sankya by Zakhar Prilepin
- Wolf Messing by Tatiana Lungin
- Good Stalin by Victor Erofeyev
- Solar Plexus by Rustam Ibragimbekov
- Don't Call me a Victim! by Dina Yafasova
- A History of Belarus by Lubov Bazan
- Children's Fashion of the Russian Empire by Alexander Vasiliev
- Boris Yeltsin - The Decade that Shook the World by Boris Minaev
- A Man Of Change - A study of the political life of Boris Yeltsin
- Gnedich by Maria Rybakova
- Marina Tsvetaeva - The Essential Poetry
- Multiple Personalities by Tatyana Shcherbina
- The Investigator by Margarita Khemlin
- Leo Tolstoy – Flight from paradise by Pavel Basinsky
- Moscow in the 1930 by Natalia Gromova
- Prisoner by Anna Nemzer
- Alpine Ballad by Vasil Bykau
- The Complete Correspondence of Hryhory
- The Tale of Aypi by Ak Welsapar
- Selected Poems by Lydia Grigorieva
- The Fantastic Worlds of Yuri Vynnychuk
- The Garden of Divine Songs and Collected Poetry of Hryhory Skovoroda
- Adventures in the Slavic Kitchen: A Book of Essays with Recipes
- Forefathers' Eve by Adam Mickiewicz
- One-Two by Igor Eliseev
- Girls, be Good by Bojan Babić
- Time of the Octopus by Anatoly Kucherena
- Tsunami by Anatoly Kurchatkin
- Pavlo Tychyna: The Complete Early Poetry Collections